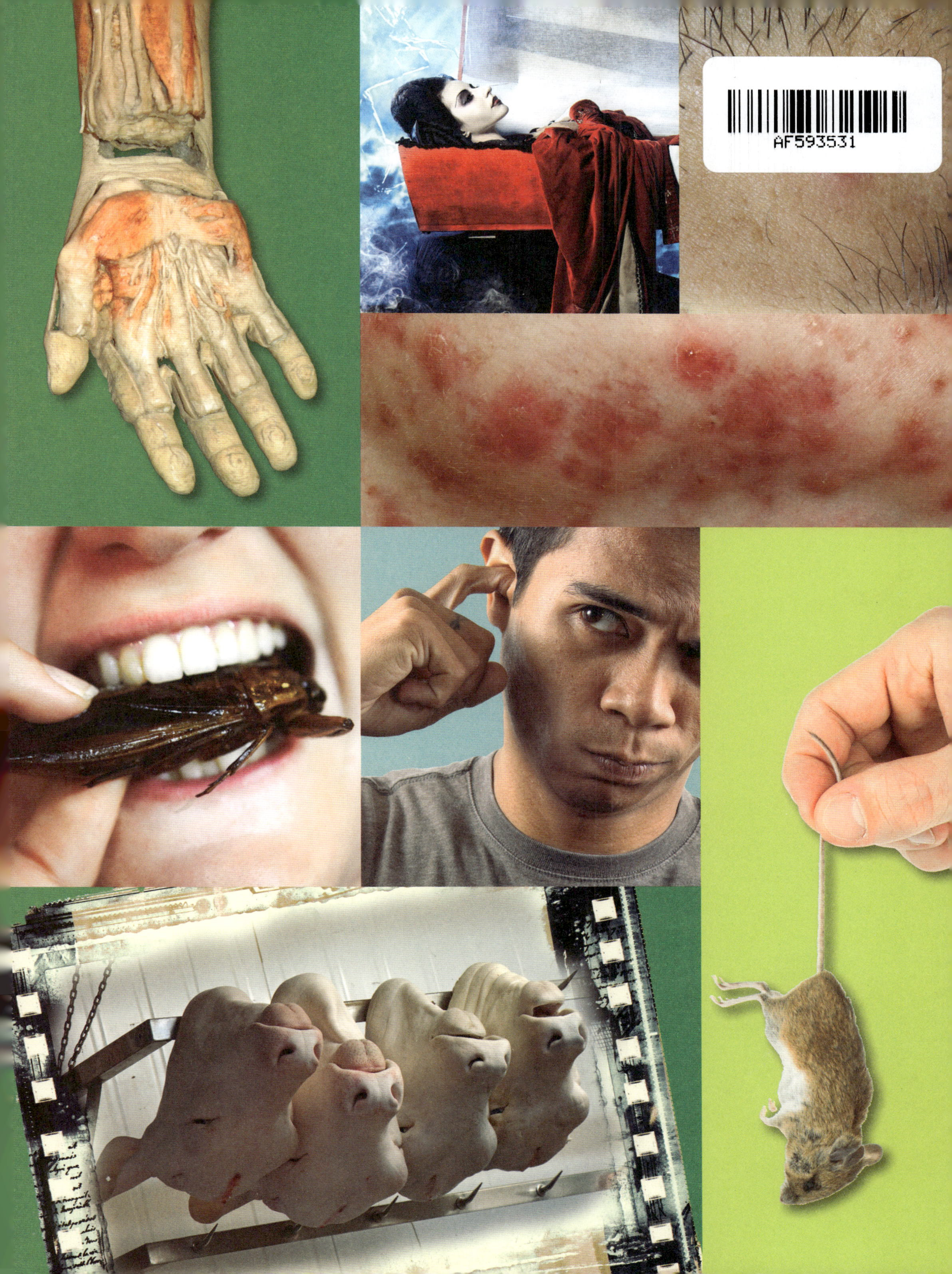
AF593531

GRUESOME FACTS

igloobooks

igloobooks

Published in 2016
by Igloo Books Ltd
Cottage Farm
Sywell
NN6 0BJ
www.igloobooks.com

HUN001 0716
2 4 6 8 10 9 7 5 3
ISBN 978-1-78440-413-0

Printed and manufactured in China

GRUESOME
FACTS

CONTENTS

SMELLIEST ANIMALS

BLOOD AND BONES

POISONOUS PLANTS

GORY GLADIATORS

DEATH RITUALS

GRUBS, WORMS AND EYEBALLS

PRESERVING BODIES

QUAKES AND WAVES

MYTHOLOGICAL MONSTERS

INDEX

SMELLIEST ANIMALS

Some animals can produce a really bad smell, especially if they feel threatened. Best keep clear of these animals if you don't want to stink, too!

OLD MUSK

The musk ox has been causing a stink since the time of the mammoths. It has lived in North America for up to 200,000 years. Although it looks like a small American bison, it is more closely related to sheep. The musk ox gets its name from the strong smell of musk in its urine that it sprays on itself and on the ground during the breeding season. Although we think the smell is terrible, female musk oxen are attracted to it!

HOW COOL!

TENTACLES

A slug may not smell too bad itself, but it has four nose-like tentacles for detecting smells, so it better not get too close to these stinky animals!

SPRAY ALERT!

The bombardier beetle is known for the foul, boiling chemicals that it shoots out of its rear. Allegedly, legendary naturalist Charles Darwin popped one in his mouth to free up a hand during a beetle-collecting expedition and experienced the stink (and probably taste!) of the beetle's spray.

If threatened, the hognose snake of North America rolls on its back and plays dead. It then gives off a foul smell and releases some excrement. This is enough to put most predators off!

AMAZING FACT!

ULTIMATE STINKER

The skunk is the most famous stinker in the world. It has stink glands in its bottom that it uses to spray a really disgusting liquid at any attacker. The liquid, which can be smelt by humans up to 1.6 km (1 mile) away, can irritate the skin of the attacker and even blind them for a time. One creature that will prey on skunks is the great horned owl, which has no sense of smell!

DID YOU KNOW?

NATIVE PERFUME

The striped polecat is a skunk-like member of the weasel family. Its anal glands can allegedly be smelled from 0.8 km (0.5 miles) away. While the animal's smell is amazing enough, even more amazing is the fact that some native peoples actually use the polecat's incredibly nasty secretions as a perfume!

SKIN SHEDDERS

Imagine if your skin was too small for you! Some animals' bodies grow, but their skin stays the same size, so they have to shed their old skin and grow a new, bigger one.

Shed skin can make a healthy snack for a lizard, as it contains valuable minerals, such as calcium. This is why lizards often nibble at their own skin when it starts to shed.

REVOLTING MOULTING

Most lizards shed their skin in patches, but when a snake slithers out of its skin, it leaves behind one whole piece (like this rattlesnake skin). Losing all the skin in one go is called 'moulting'. Animals usually stop eating for at least a few days to prepare for a moult.

WATCH OUT!

DEADLY RATTLE

The rattles at the end of a rattlesnake's tail are made up of layers of shed, dry skin that make a noise when shaken. The noise warns other animals to keep clear of the snake and its deadly bite.

SKINNED

Snakeskins are often used to make handbags, wallets and shoes. Moulted skin is too thin to be used, so snakes are kept in farms where first, they are starved, so their skins loosen and then they are pumped with water so the skins stretch. Finally, they are killed.

PLAYING DEAD

Spiders don't have a bony skeleton like us, instead they have a really strong skin called an exoskeleton. The exoskeleton doesn't grow, so when a spider gets bigger, its old skin cracks open and the new, soft-skinned spider steps out. If you spot a tarantula lying on its back, beware! Although it may look dead, it might actually just be moulting.

When a young insect, such as a cicada, turns into an adult, it goes through a big body change called a metamorphosis. The old skin splits open and the adult simply climbs out!

DID YOU KNOW?

SLITHER AND SLIDE

Baby garter snakes get a new skin within minutes of being born. The moult can take less than five minutes once it has started. The paper-thin old skin is left behind as the snake slides away. It's like pulling a leg out of a long sock!

ANIMAL SLIME

What's the point of slime? It may look and feel disgusting, but slime is very useful. Without it, some animals simply couldn't survive.

GOO IS GOOD!

Slime helps snails and slugs to slither along the ground, over stones and prickles and up walls. Slime is so tough that a slug can even glide along a razor blade without getting hurt! Slugs dry out very easily, but a thick coat of slime helps them to stay moist. Snails have hard shells, so they don't dry out as easily as slugs, but they still need slime to help them slide.

MEAT EATER

Most slugs are happy to eat vegetables and other plants, but some giant slugs, such as Spanish slugs, also graze on dead animals. When groups of them feed on roadkill, their slime is slimy enough to send cars sideways!

AMAZING!

SNAIL TREATS

Snail slime has been used to make spot creams and to treat wounds. Snail eggs are even on the menu in some restaurants. People say they are a bit like caviar, but have a more 'earthy' taste!

Hagfish don't have spines and they don't even have jaws, but they do have super-strong, super-stretchy slime. Their skin makes mucus filled with lots of threads. When the mucus combines with water, it expands in size and stickiness, making it almost impossible for sharks to bite the fish.

MEGA-SLIME

You know you've got giant African land snails living in your garden because they leave huge slime trails and long, ribbon-like poops! Each snail grows to 20 cm (8 in) long and eats flowers, vegetables and fruit. Little worms live inside these snails, a single snail may have thousands of worms wriggling away inside it. In some places, the snails are considered a real treat and are eaten raw.

DID YOU KNOW?

USEFUL?

To scrape off old slime, a hagfish ties itself in a knot, then slides the knot down its body. Scientists hope to use the hagfish's slime recipe to make clothes and even bulletproof vests.

BLOODSUCKERS

Drinking blood may seem disgusting, but it is an almost perfect food. It contains sugar for energy, water, iron and muscle-building protein.

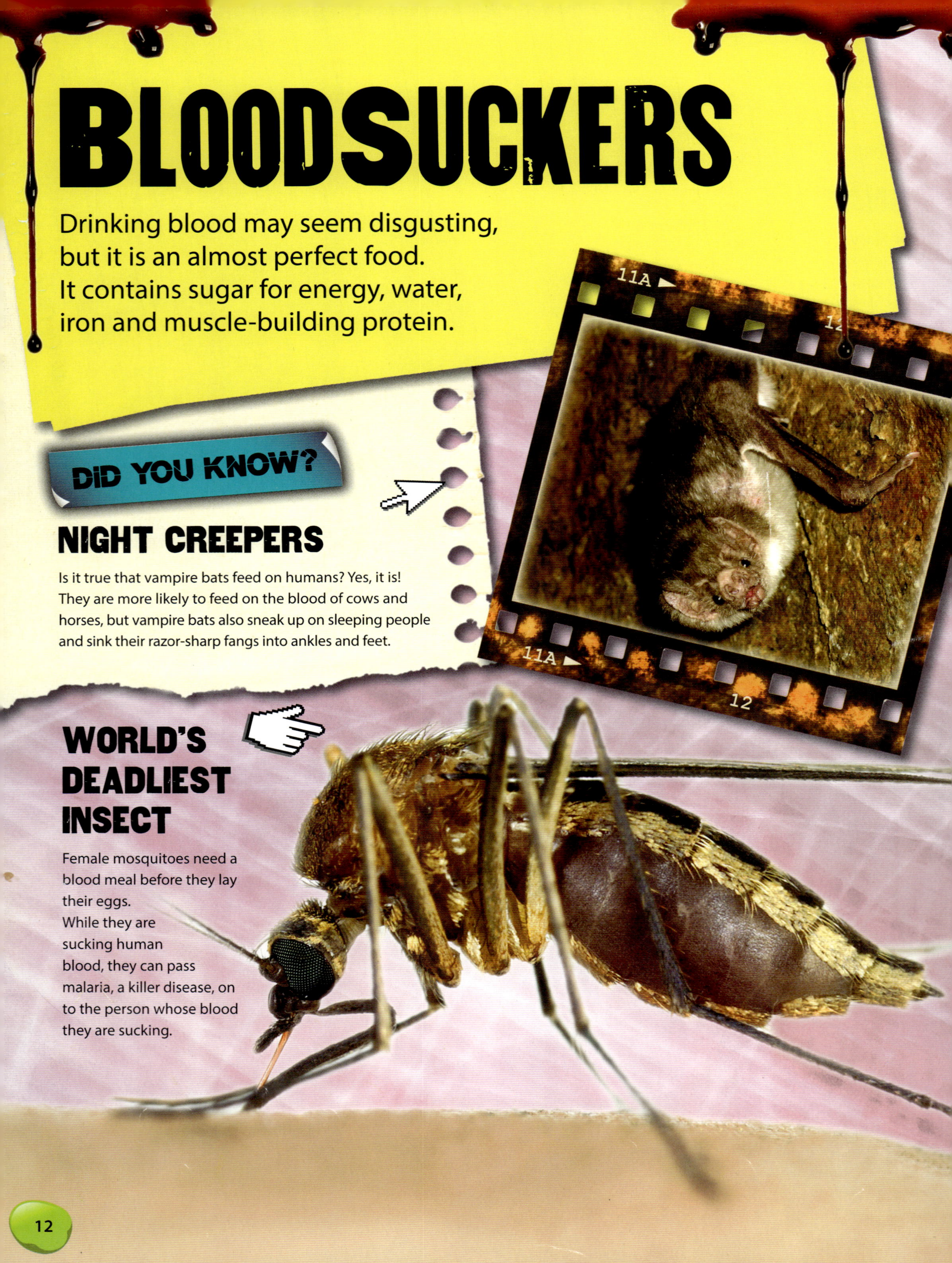

DID YOU KNOW?

NIGHT CREEPERS

Is it true that vampire bats feed on humans? Yes, it is! They are more likely to feed on the blood of cows and horses, but vampire bats also sneak up on sleeping people and sink their razor-sharp fangs into ankles and feet.

WORLD'S DEADLIEST INSECT

Female mosquitoes need a blood meal before they lay their eggs. While they are sucking human blood, they can pass malaria, a killer disease, on to the person whose blood they are sucking.

TERRIBLE TICKS

This nasty-looking bug is a member of the spider family and it has a taste for blood. Ticks bury their jaws into a victim's flesh and suck out the blood with a straw-like mouthpart. While they feed, ticks can pass deadly diseases to their victims.

YUCK!

BIG FEEDERS

Leeches are soft, squidgy, slimy bloodsuckers. They slice through skin using three blade-like jaws and suck up the blood that pours out. Leeches can drink five times their own bodyweight in blood. They can also store lots of blood in their bodies, some of them only need to feed twice a year!

COOL FACT!

SNEAKY

Animals that drink blood are called haematophages (heem-at-oh-fay-jes). Many blood feeders are able to stop the blood from clotting, so it keeps flowing. They also pour painkillers into their victims, so they can't feel their skin being broken.

JUMP FOR JOY

Fleas scurry around on a victim's skin, hiding between strands of hair. They pierce the skin and suck up the blood that pools there. Once they have fed, fleas drop off their victims' bodies and snooze in their beds or nests instead. When it's time for tea, a flea can jump back on to its host using its super-springy legs. It can leap 200 times its own body length!

PESKY PARASITES

Meet the nastiest, most disgusting animals on the planet. These creepy creatures have such gruesome lifestyles, you may never feel the same way about wildlife again!

UNWELCOME VISITORS

Animals that live on, or inside, another animal are called parasites. They get their food from the other animal, which is called the 'host'. Over time, the parasite makes the host ill, or even kills it.

BOT FLIES

Adult bot flies drop their larvae on to the skin of an animal, such as a horse, or a human. The larvae burrow into the host's flesh, feeding on it and causing nasty wounds and infections that weep and ooze all the time. In horses, the larvae eventually pass out in the animal's dung. Adult bot flies emerge from the dung 2-8 weeks later.

MINI MONSTERS

Many parasites are too small to see, but they can still be deadly. Toxoplasmas are tiny creatures that live in rats, mice, cats and people. When they are inside rats, these pests make their hosts fearless and especially keen on cats. They love the smell of cat wee! As the rats get closer to the cats, the cats are able to catch and eat them and they become infected, too.

EXPLODING FLY

If you find a splattered fly, it may be the victim of a type of fungus that grew inside the fly's body, dissolving all of its body bits from the inside out! When it's ready, the fungus makes the fly explode and splatter.

LIVER FLUKE

Liver fluke worms lay eggs that hatch in water. The young swim about until they find a water snail, which they burrow into. When they are ready, the young flukes burst of the snail's flesh and se some juicy green gra or cow to come (the sheep o animal's li

POISONOUS PLANTS

Plants give us food, clothing and shelter, but some plants pack a powerful punch. Their gruesome poisons can make us very sick… or worse!

DEAD MAN'S BELLS

Foxgloves look like perfect garden flowers, but their common name of dead man's bells gives a clue to their deadly nature. They have a poison that affects the heart and can cause a heart attack. People have used them to make heart medicines, but also to commit murder!

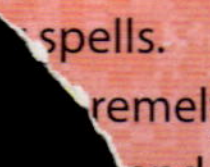

spells.
remely
end,
fro

DEADLY BEANS

The deadliest plant in the world is the castor bean plant. As the large, spiny seed pods dry out in the sun, they split open and the beans shoot out with considerable force and fly through the air. The beans contain the poison ricin. Eating just a few beans would kill a person in minutes.

Never eat the berries from a deadly nightshade plant. They contain a chemical called atropine that can cause breathing problems, terrible headaches and death.

LETHAL LEAVES

Hemlocks look harmless, but some types are deadly to animals and humans. Victims can die agonizing deaths within just a few hours of eating the leaves.

AMAZING!

TOXIC TREE

The manchineel tree grows throughout the Florida Everglades, Central America and the Caribbean. Eating its fruit can kill you, smoke from burning its wood can cause blindness and just standing under it in a rainstorm and getting splashed by the water running off its leaves can cause rashes and itching.

STINKY PLANTS

Imagine the smell of rotting socks, foul drains, dead bodies and sweaty gym shoes. These are just some of the disgusting smells that plants can make.

STINKY TREAT

Orang-utans love to dine on durian fruit. The smell from this juicy stinker has been described as a mix between rotting fish and poo, but lots of jungle animals adore it. They know that the stink comes from the prickly rind and that the fleshy fruit inside is soft, juicy and very tasty.

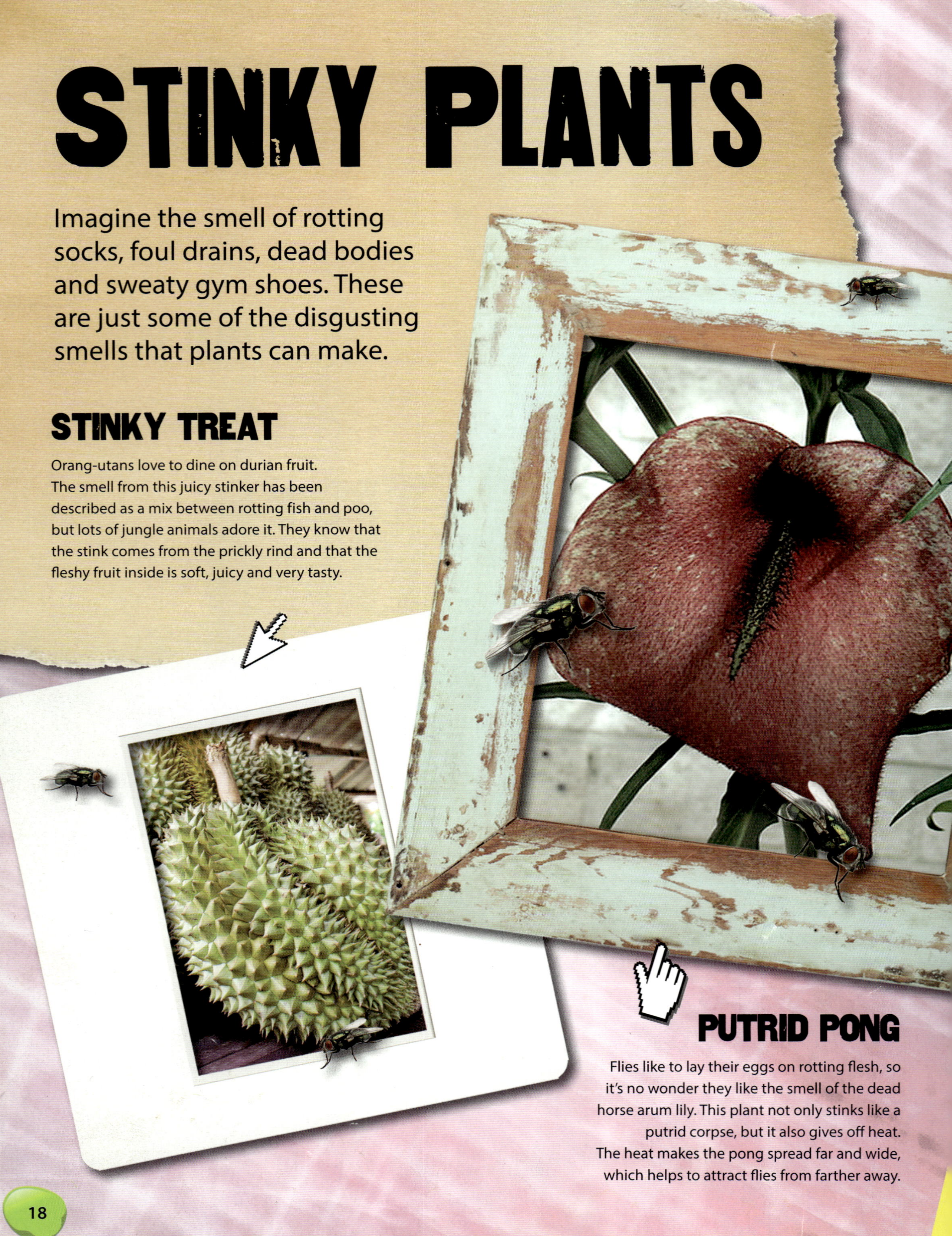

PUTRID PONG

Flies like to lay their eggs on rotting flesh, so it's no wonder they like the smell of the dead horse arum lily. This plant not only stinks like a putrid corpse, but it also gives off heat. The heat makes the pong spread far and wide, which helps to attract flies from farther away.

AMAZING!

UPSIDE-DOWN TREE

The freaky-looking baobab tree is also called the upside-down tree, because when bare, its huge trunk and thick branches look more like roots. Baobabs have huge, white flowers that smell quite sweet until they turn brown, when they start to stink. The rotting, musty smell attracts bats, which pollinate the flowers.

CORPSE FLOWER

Plants need insects to help them grow seeds. To attract them, some plants make sweet smells, while others make a foul stink. Titan arum flowers, known in Indonesia as 'corpse flowers', smell of rotting meat and that's a smell that lots of flies find too tempting to resist. The flowers grow to a record-breaking 3 m (10 ft) tall, so their stench can spread far across the forest.

DID YOU KNOW?

STRANGE SMELLS

A titan arum's foul smell can make people nearby feel sick, but other arums smell of bananas or freshly chopped carrots.

FLESH-EATING PLANTS

Most plants make their own food, but some prefer to 'eat' food and they have some gross ways of getting their meals!

SNAP TRAPS

The Venus flytrap is the most famous of all mean, green, meat-eating plants. When a fly lands on the soft, fleshy 'traps', it can wander about happily, until it touches one of the trigger hairs. Then, slam! The trap shuts, capturing the fly inside and its body is soon turned into a juicy, gloopy mush.

STICKY TRICKS

The pretty red stalks on this sundew plant are tipped with glue. Bugs land on the stalks, thinking they are in for a treat of sugary nectar, but instead find themselves trapped. The more they wriggle, the faster they stick.

FLY SOUP

The long cups on pitcher plants are made from rolled-up leaves. Flies are tempted into the cups by their bright shades and sweet smells. Inside the cups, the flies drown in a pool of water and flesh-dissolving chemicals. The plant then absorbs the goodness from the "fly soup".

AMAZING!

FROGS' FEET

Some pitcher plants get extra goodness from animal droppings that fall in to their cups. Others trap frogs and turn them into frog soup. All that remains of the frogs are their feet as for some reason, the skin on their feet doesn't dissolve!

COOL FACT!

NICE AND SLOW

It can take up to 10 days for a Venus flytrap to digest its meal.

QUICK AS A FLASH

Bladderworts grow in ponds and are the fastest killers in the animal kingdom. Their traps can slam shut on a mosquito larva in less than 0.02 seconds.

STINGERS AND STRANGLERS

Some plants have weapons to defend themselves against animal attack. Others attack and kill other plants.

A strangler fig grows up and around another rainforest tree, slowly strangling it to death. After the big tree has died and rotted away, the strangler fig is left standing as a hollow tower.

DON'T TOUCH!

The leaves of stinging nettles are armed with tiny hairs tipped with beads of glass (silica). When a hair is touched, the glass breaks off and the end of the hair injects a cocktail of poisons. Some of the chemicals give you pain, some make your skin itchy and swollen and others make the pain and itchiness worse!

WATCH OUT!

LIGHT ALERT

The sap of the giant hogweed plant, which is often grown in parks and gardens in Europe and North America, can give you a nasty rash and blisters that scar for years. However, the sting only takes effect if you touch the plant and then let the sun shine on your skin.

DID YOU KNOW?

DON'T LOOK NOW!

The blinding tree, or 'blind your eye', grows in mangrove forests and swamps in many tropical parts of the world. The sap from the blinding tree can make a person go blind. Every part of the plant is poisonous and must not be eaten.

RUNAWAY ROOTS

Like a massive, slow-moving monster, this huge tree (*Tetrameles nudiflora*) is slowly taking over the Ta Prohm temple ruins in Cambodia, Southeast Asia. The giant buttress roots of this type of tree can grow up to 6 m (20 ft) tall, while the tree itself can reach a staggering 45 m (147 ft) tall, about as tall as 26 men standing on each other's shoulders!

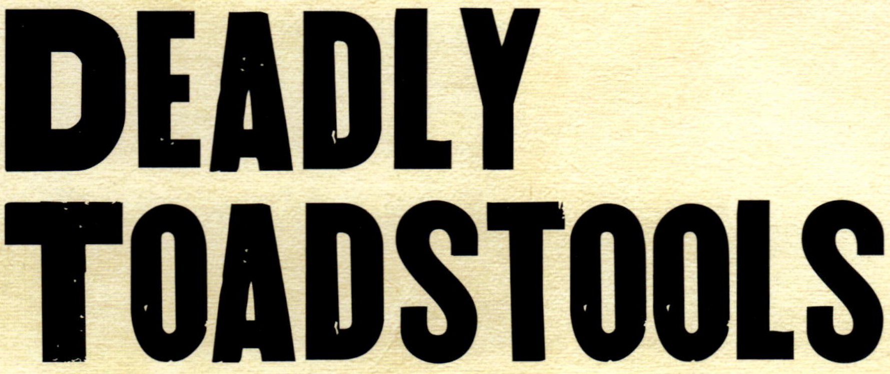

DEADLY TOADSTOOLS

Do you think mushrooms and toadstools are plants? Think again, because they are more like animals. They belong in a group of living things called fungi (say, "fun-ghee").

AMAZING!

WHY ISN'T A FUNGUS A PLANT?

Fungi do not make their own food. They feed on other living things, or on dead animals and plants.

OBSCURE ORIGINS

Toadstools and mushrooms are the same thing. They are the parts of a fungus in which the spores (seeds) grow. The word 'toadstool' dates back to the 14th century and is generally used to mean a poisonous mushroom. Toads were regarded as being very poisonous.

Death caps look very similar to mushrooms that are fine to eat and that spells bad news for mushroom pickers. Eating just half of a death cap mushroom would be enough to kill an adult.

ANGEL OF DEATH

The pretty white caps of this toadstool look like little umbrellas, but this fungus is called the 'angel of death' and with a name like that, you know it's best to stay away from it! Eating it can have deadly results. First, a victim is violently ill and empties out his guts. Then his liver is slowly destroyed. The chances of survival are small.

RED FOR DANGER!

The red cap of this toadstool spells danger. It is a fly agaric and it is filled with poison. Anyone who eats a fly agaric will find that the poison makes them sweat and dribble, a lot! It also makes them confused and they may imagine seeing things that aren't really there.

FACT FILE

We have tiny fungi growing on our skin. Sometimes they grow too much and cause foul skin conditions, such as athlete's foot.

Mould is a type of fungus. It makes bread go green, apples rot and turns old meat toxic and smelly.

Fly agarics were once used to make a potion for killing flies and other insects.

BLOOD AND BONES

The human body sometimes suffers some gruesome wounds, but it has an amazing ability to heal itself.

BILLIONS OF BEATS

If you die at the age of 75, your busy heart will have beaten about 3 billion times. It beats at least once a second, sending blood around your body and back to your lungs to pick up more life-giving oxygen. A body holds about 5 litres (1 gallon) of blood. Each day, about 15,000 litres (3,300 gallons) of blood pass through the heart.

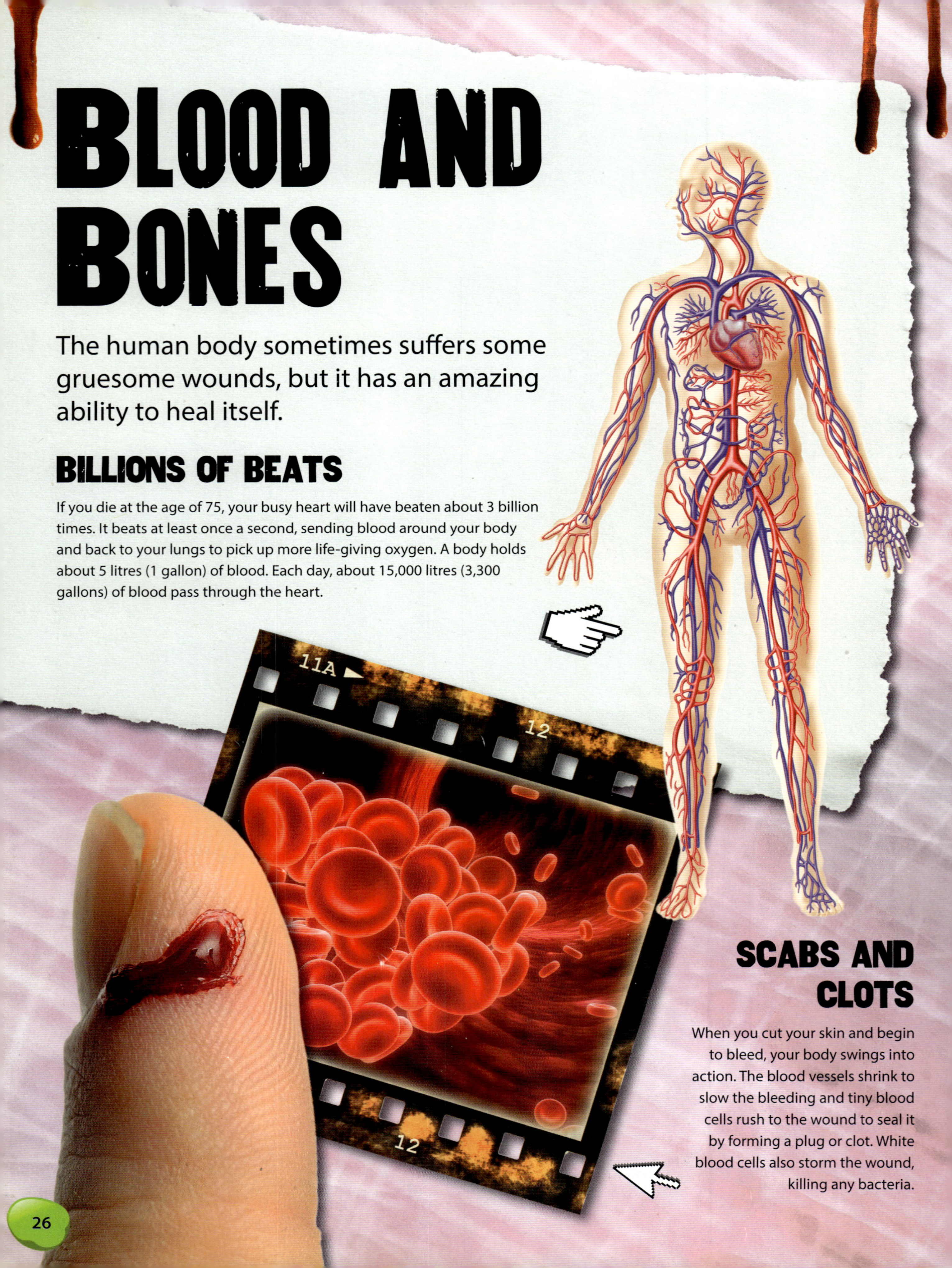

SCABS AND CLOTS

When you cut your skin and begin to bleed, your body swings into action. The blood vessels shrink to slow the bleeding and tiny blood cells rush to the wound to seal it by forming a plug or clot. White blood cells also storm the wound, killing any bacteria.

JELLY BONES

Bones aren't completely hard. They have a soft, spongy bit inside called the marrow, which looks a bit like jelly. Bone marrow makes 173 billion new blood cells every day!

IN A TWIST

People with flexible joints can turn their bodies back to front, bend their fingers right back and pull their arms out of their sockets. Gross!

DID YOU KNOW?

SNAPPING BONES

If you break a bone, blood will flow into the broken bit and form a clot. Soft cartilage, which is like bendy bone, grows over the break and new bone begins to set. The break can be repaired in less than six weeks.

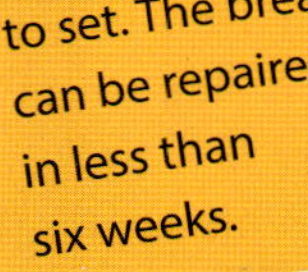

SQUISHY NOSE

Your nose is made of cartilage, not hard bone and that's why you can squish it with your fingers.

DISAPPEARING BONES

Babies have about 300 bones, but there are 206 bones in an adult body, connected by 400 joints. Do babies lose 94 bones? No, their bones just fuse together to make fewer bones.

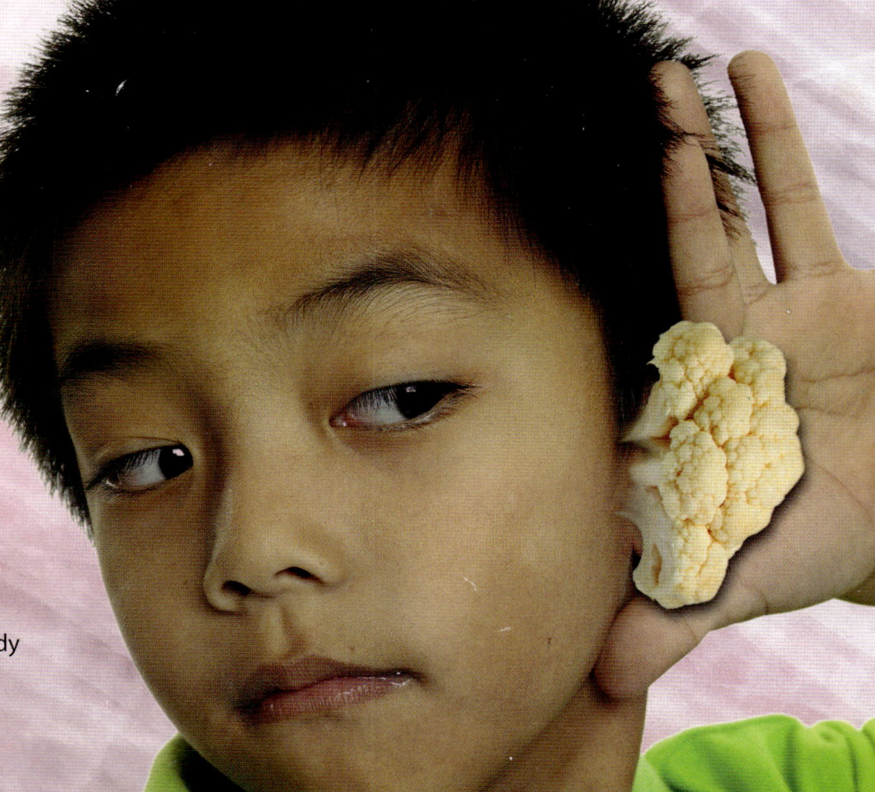

VEGGIE HEAD

Scars form when a wound is too deep to heal with a simple scab. Repeated wounds to one area of the body can cause life-long damage, such as cauliflower ear. This is a condition in which the ear develops nasty lumps and bumps that won't go away. People who play contact sports are most at risk.

DIGESTION

One enormous tube runs through your body, from your mouth to your bottom. It takes food on an amazing journey of disgusting digestion.

WE NEED FOOD

You are what you eat, but the reason you don't look like a burger and fries, or slippery noodles is that your body does a magical trick with food and turns it into something else. This process takes place in your digestive system, where food is broken down and turned into energy and other important stuff to repair your body and help it grow. Poo is what's left over!

BIG BURPS!

Look out! Gas is brewing, stewing and fizzing in your gut. As the bubbles grow, there's only one way for them to go, up and out! We burp when gases build up in our stomachs after swallowing air during a meal, or from drinking fizzy drinks. A burp is noisy because the gas makes the seal between your stomach and throat vibrate. Unfortunately, if that seal is weak you may bring up some food with a burp and that's sick.

AMAZING!

MMM, TASTY!

Intestine and stomach walls are covered with a thick slime to stop them from digesting themselves. Even so, one million stomach cells are turned into stomach soup every minute.

GRUESOME GUTS

Your intestines, or guts, are the long, sausage-like tubes that run from your stomach to your bottom. They are 8 m (26 ft) long, which is hard to imagine when you look at your belly! The intestines are where the gruesome job of making poo takes place. First, all the goodness is taken out of the food as it passes through and then the waste is passed out of your tail end about 12 hours after your meal.

GROWLING

Sometimes your stomach makes an embarrassing rumbling or growling noise. This happens when pockets of air and gas get squeezed along with the gooey mix of food in your digestive system.

SOUPY STOMACH

Once food is swallowed, it is forced down into the stomach, where a foul soup of burning acid awaits it. The stomach churns the food around every 20 seconds or so, making slurpy noises as it mixes it in with the acid. This mashes the food, so it's small and soft enough to go on to the guts.

ZITS, BOILS AND SORES

As well as beastly bacteria, the skin plays host to viruses and tiny fungi, too and these can cause us no end of trouble!

TERRIBLE TEENS

When children begin to turn into adults, they start to grow thicker hair, and more of it, and their skin makes extra sebum. The thicker hairs and greasy sebum block up the tiny holes (pores) in the skin and that's when the zit trouble begins!

WARTS

Viruses are the zombies of the natural world because they are sort of alive, but not quite, and they are difficult to destroy. Warts are caused by viruses that make the skin grow into lots of rough, hard layers that build up into big bumps. They are harmless, but annoying. Warts that grow on feet are called verrucas.

AMAZING!

ACNE DIARY

1. Sweat and sebum block up the skin's tiny pores and can't escape. They build up under the skin, forming little bumps.
2. Bacteria start to feast. (If no bacteria feed on the sebum, you get a blackhead.)
3. An infection builds up and the bumps turn into mini-volcanoes, spots or zits!
4. White blood cells storm in to kill the bacteria and make lots of oozy, gloopy pus.
5. Pressure builds up and the zit erupts, forcing out the bacteria, blood and pus. Gross!

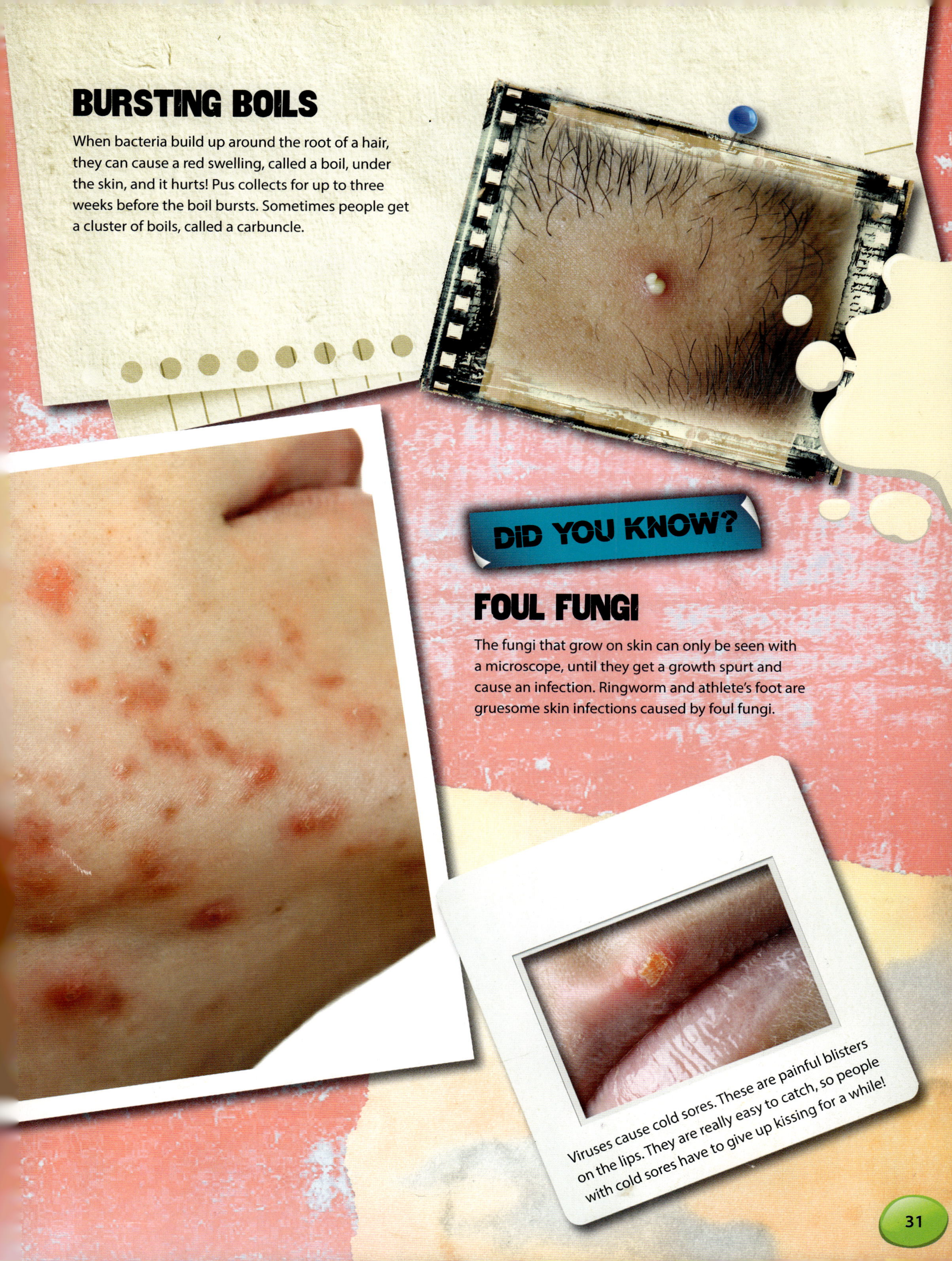

BURSTING BOILS

When bacteria build up around the root of a hair, they can cause a red swelling, called a boil, under the skin, and it hurts! Pus collects for up to three weeks before the boil bursts. Sometimes people get a cluster of boils, called a carbuncle.

DID YOU KNOW?

FOUL FUNGI

The fungi that grow on skin can only be seen with a microscope, until they get a growth spurt and cause an infection. Ringworm and athlete's foot are gruesome skin infections caused by foul fungi.

Viruses cause cold sores. These are painful blisters on the lips. They are really easy to catch, so people with cold sores have to give up kissing for a while!

THE SMELLY BITS

Let's face it, most of the odours that come from a person's body don't smell too good.

CHEESY SHOES

The palms of our hands and soles of our feet make lots of sweat. If we trap the sweat on our feet in socks and shoes, we are creating the perfect place for bacteria to grow and make our feet smelly. Some things increase the amount we sweat, such as exercise, eating curry and drinking tea or coffee, but there's one part of us that never sweats, and that's our lips.

DOG BREATH

Eating garlic and onions can make your breath smell of... garlic and onions! Real bad breath is much nastier, because it's mostly caused by bacteria farts. The bacteria feed on leftover bits of food stuck between teeth and on the tongue and they make foul-smelling gases.

WHO DID THAT?

As food travels through the guts, it's worked on by helpful bacteria that break it down so that the body can take out the goodness. Unfortunately, the bacteria make lots of gas while they work and that gas has to escape. When it leaves the body, the gas often makes a loud noise and a foul smell and that's a fart!

ARMPIT DISASTER

Sweat cools us down as it evaporates on our skin, but under our arms it gets trapped. Bacteria thrive in this dark, damp environment and start to break the sweat down. It's this breakdown that creates an unpleasant smell. If we wash the bacteria off, we wash the smell away, too.

COOL FACT!

DON'T TRY THIS!

Farts contain a gas called methane. It burns really easily if you set a match to it (but we don't recommend you try this at home!).

MORE DEADLY DISEASES

Deadly diseases can spread quickly, causing people to have gruesome symptoms and die agonizing deaths.

PLAGUE VICTIMS

The plague is rare nowadays, but it has caused hundreds of millions of deaths in the past. Victims get ill, coughing up their lungs, developing big black lumps under the skin and bleeding from every hole. Sufferers can die a terrible death within just four days of catching the plague. In the 17th and 18th centuries, plague doctors wore beak-like masks filled with herbs to protect them from the putrid air that they believed was a cause of the plague.

MAD AND BAD

If you hate baths and often have spit dribbling out of your mouth, you are exhibiting two signs of rabies, a foul disease that is caught when an animal infected with rabies bites you. It affects the brain, driving you crazy and making it unbearably painful to swallow, which leads to a fear of water.

AMAZING!

BAD BACTERIA

Known as the Black Death, plague is caused by bacteria that live inside rat fleas, but it easily spreads to people. Once a person has the plague, the bacteria grow quickly in their blood. Within a few days they may have a billion bacteria in every drop of blood.

Tetanus bacteria make a deadly toxin that makes muscles contract and jaws freeze, which is why the disease is sometimes called lockjaw. You can get it from puncture wounds, such as those made by rusty nails.

SCURVY

What happens if you don't eat fruit and vegetables? Your teeth fall out, your skin can turn purple and yellow, you get very sick with an illness called scurvy and then you die! Why? Because fruit and vegetables contain Vitamin C, which your body needs to make collagen, the really important stuff that holds your bones and skin together.

COOL FACT!

POOR DIET

Sailors suffered from scurvy when they were at sea, because a diet of rum and maggot-filled biscuits was low in Vitamin C. Often the sailors got better when they were given lemon or lime juice to drink, or fresh fruit to eat.

GORY GLADIATORS

Imagine being sent out in front of a yelling crowd to kill someone, or be killed! That was the fate of a gladiator in ancient Rome.

COOL FACT!

SWORD SWAP

A gladiator with a sword might fight an unarmed opponent. If he won, he had to fight next time without a sword.

KILLING SCHOOLS

Gladiators were trained in special fighting schools. Most were prisoners of war, criminals or slaves. Some gladiators wore armour so heavy they could hardly walk. Others fought almost naked. There were a few women fighters, too.

NO PAPER!

Nervous gladiators probably needed the toilet before a fight. The Romans did not use toilet paper. Instead they used a water-soaked sponge on the end of a stick!

AMAZING!

FIGHTER'S FOOD

In training, gladiators ate mostly starchy foods and vegetables. Trainers fed them spoonfuls of ash to make their bones stronger.

CHOOSE YOUR WEAPON

Some gladiators were chasers, they ran around the arena with a sword and shield. Some had two swords. A tricky fighter was the *retiarius*, who threw a net to entangle his opponent, then stabbed him with a long, three-pronged fork, called a trident.

All gladiators swore to fight to the death. If a fighter tried to run away, the crowd would jeer. He might then be tortured to amuse them, before being killed.

THUMB SIGNAL

If a gladiator was wounded and the crowd wanted him to live, they would wave their scarves and hands. The emperor then signalled his fate, but no one is sure whether he put his thumb up or down if the gladiator was to die. If the sign was "die", the wounded man was killed and his body dragged out of the arena.

FIGHTING BLIND

Roman crowds always liked something new. Sometimes a gladiator was pitched against a bear or a tiger. Sometimes two gangs of gladiators fought each other. A gladiator might even be made to wear a helmet with no eye holes, so he could not see what he was trying to hit.

HORRID ROMAN HABITS

Rich Romans enjoyed the good life, but some Roman habits and tastes seem gruesome to us today. They could be quite disgusting!

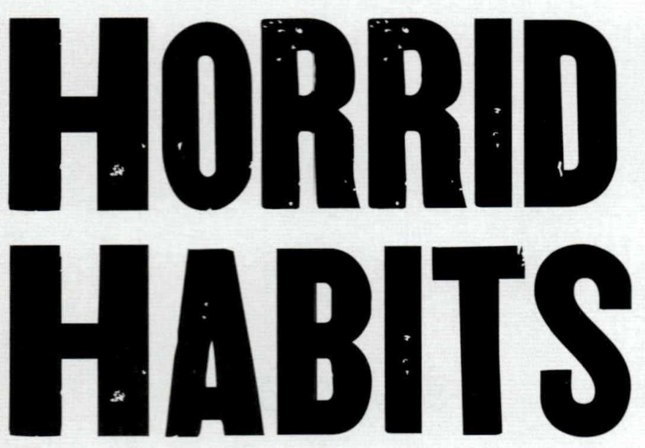

SNAIL DELIGHT

The Romans liked to fatten snails on a diet of milk and salt and then fry them as a delicacy. Snails are still a popular dish in France.

YOU MUST BE JOKING!

Roman cooks amused dinner guests by creating joke dishes, for example by serving up a roast hare with birds' wings attached, to make it look like a miniature Pegasus (the fabled winged horse). A very popular titbit was a dormouse, stuffed or dipped in honey and rolled in poppy seeds.

The Romans had a very popular sauce, which was found in almost every kitchen. It was made from smelly fish guts that were salted and dried in the sun.

HUMAN CANDLES

The Emperor Nero regularly held vile orgies at his palace, the Golden House, in Rome. Here, guests were given special bowls to vomit into after they had eaten to excess. They were also made to witness one of his most barbaric acts. Nero had Christian prisoners tied to wooden stakes, smeared with tar and set alight to burn as human candles.

DID YOU KNOW?

LETHAL LEAD

The Romans liked to drink wine sweetened with a syrup, called 'defrutum', which was made from grapes fermented in lead pots. Lead also leached from the glazes of pottery and from lead piping used to carry water. Many Romans suffered from severe lead poisoning as a result. Symptoms included painful gout and even madness.

WASH DAY

People in ancient times did not have washing powder. Instead, they made soap from ashes and collected wee in pots to use on wash day, as a soaking bleach to whiten clothes. Wee was also used by leather-makers, who collected it by the cartload.

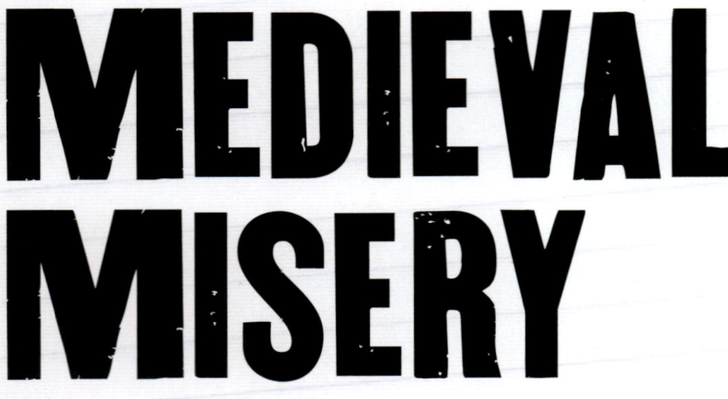

MEDIEVAL MISERY

Life was tough in Medieval times. Homes were cold, the streets stank, disease was a constant concern and punishments were harsh.

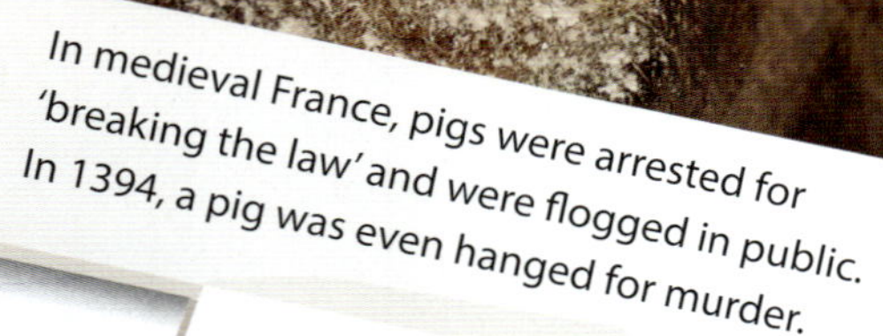

In medieval France, pigs were arrested for 'breaking the law' and were flogged in public. In 1394, a pig was even hanged for murder.

DOG AND DUCK

Medieval inns named 'The Dog and Duck' held gruesome duck-baiting events. A duck with a clipped wing was released onto a pond, where it was chased by dogs. Its only escape was to dive underwater. The owner of the dog that caught the duck in the least amount of time got a prize. If the duck escaped, the dog's owner had to pay the local innkeeper.

DID YOU KNOW?

GRIM PRISON

The most feared London jail in the Middle Ages was Newgate Prison. People called it a 'tomb for the living'. Prisoners were chained together in damp, dark, cold cells with no heat, no bedding and no toilets. More people died there from sickness than were ever hanged.

ORDEAL BY FIRE

A person accused of a crime might be made to suffer an 'ordeal by fire'. This involved walking three steps carrying a piece of red-hot iron. The person's hand was then bandaged. If, after three days, the skin had not blistered, the person was judged to be innocent, but if there were blisters, the accused was found guilty and likely put to death.

DID YOU KNOW?

PUBLIC HUMILIATION

A fish-seller accused of selling rotten fish had to walk about with a stinking dead fish tied around his neck. A bad baker was dragged about on a wooden sledge, while a bad priest had to sit on a horse facing the tail and wearing a paper crown, while people jeered at him.

AMAZING!

DIRTY STREETS

The streets of Medieval towns were not places to linger. There was no sewage system, so toilet waste was simply thrown out onto the streets, the stench would have knocked you over! Rotten food was also thrown out, to be eaten by roaming pigs or the numerous rats. Not surprisingly, life expectancy for a poor person in a town was short.

TOOTHACHE

Toothache was a real misery in Medieval times. With no effective painkillers, people suffered in agony. When they could stand it no longer, they had their rotten teeth yanked out by tooth-pullers, who did a roaring trade at the weekly markets.

PUNISHMENTS

Punishments were often cruel and bloody. Painful torture was the fate of many prisoners in dark dungeons and loathsome cells.

IRON MAIDEN

The Iron Maiden looked a bit like a coffin or an Egyptian mummy case, but it was armed with vicious spikes. The helpless prisoner strapped inside would see the spikes closing in as the doors were shut. The Iron Maiden's final embrace was deadly!

TRAITORS ON SHOW

The heads of executed traitors were stuck on pikes (spear-like weapons) or poles for crows to peck at and crowds to mock. Guy Fawkes and the other Gunpowder plotters of 1605 ended up in this sorry state.

ON THE RACK

Invented in the 1400s, the rack was a torture instrument used in the Tower of London and other prisons to extract information. The victim was tied to a wooden frame by the arms and legs and was painfully stretched until he gasped what his torturers wanted to hear, or until his bones and joints shattered.

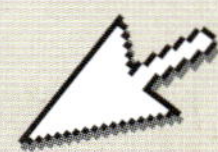

DID YOU KNOW?

TRAPPED!

The Little Ease cell in the Tower of London was so small that a prisoner could not stand up or lie full length inside it without touching the walls or ceiling.

WATCH OUT!

THUMBS DOWN

Thumb screws were simple but effective. The victim's thumb was put into a clamp like a nutcracker and was crushed. If he didn't talk, there was always the other thumb, and then the fingers...

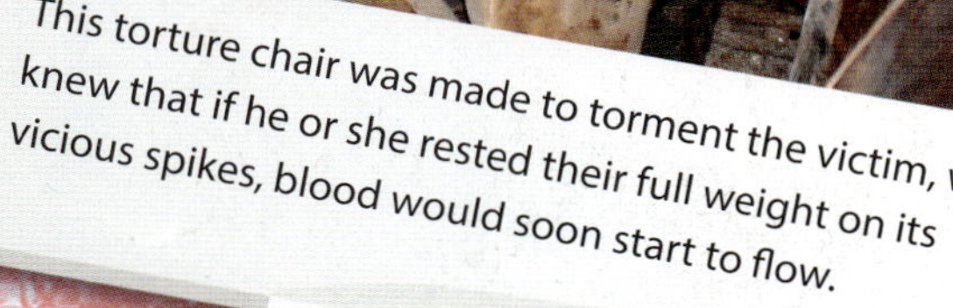

This torture chair was made to torment the victim, who knew that if he or she rested their full weight on its vicious spikes, blood would soon start to flow.

FRENCH FRIGHTS

The years 1789-1815 were dramatic for France. First came the French Revolution, famed for its executions, then came Emperor Napoleon, who fought endless battles.

DID YOU KNOW?

OFF WITH HIS HEAD!

The French Revolution began in 1789, after a mob stormed the Bastille prison in Paris. The old government was overthrown and France was torn apart as nobles fled abroad and people took to the streets. King Louis XVI was imprisoned in 1792 and beheaded on the guillotine in January 1793.

REIGN OF TERROR

The French Revolution turned really nasty in September 1793. In October, the revolutionaries, led by Maximilien de Robespierre, executed Queen Marie Antoinette, who they blamed for the country's financial problems. After the queen's execution, hundreds of other 'enemies of the people' were sent to their deaths.

MADAME LA GUILLOTINE

The guillotine was developed by Dr Joseph Guillotin to provide a quick, humane and 'classless' method of execution, suitable for rich or poor. It was first tested on animals and then, in April 1792, on a highwayman. The spectators were disappointed, as death by guillotine was so quick!

DEATH OF ROBESPIERRE

Maximilien de Robespierre was the most bloodthirsty of all the French revolutionary leaders. He declared that even friends must die if they opposed the Revolution. When the order for his arrest was finally made, in July 1794, he tried to shoot himself, but managed instead to shatter his jaw. The next day, still bleeding and screaming as his bandages were torn off, he was guillotined.

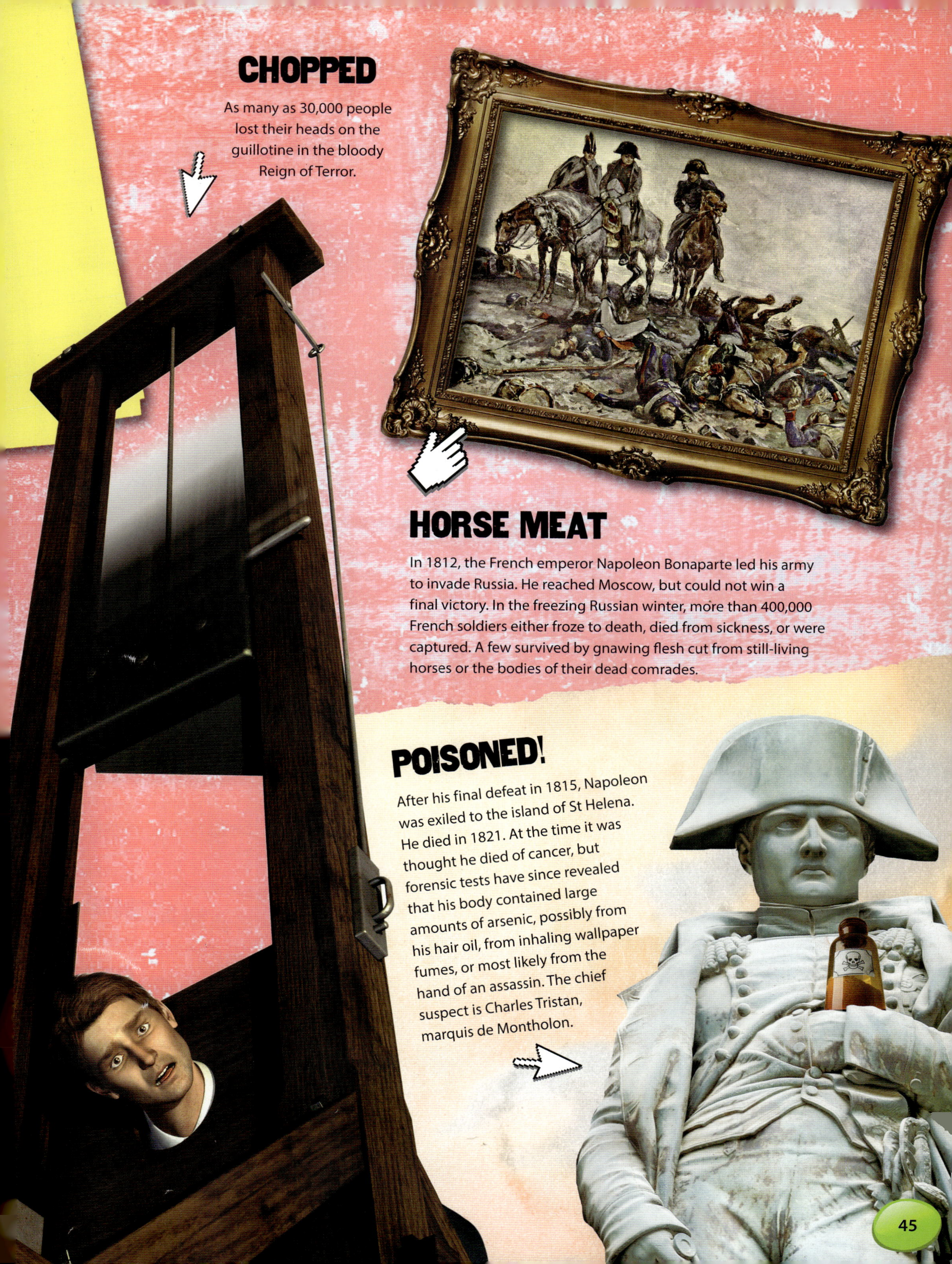

CHOPPED

As many as 30,000 people lost their heads on the guillotine in the bloody Reign of Terror.

HORSE MEAT

In 1812, the French emperor Napoleon Bonaparte led his army to invade Russia. He reached Moscow, but could not win a final victory. In the freezing Russian winter, more than 400,000 French soldiers either froze to death, died from sickness, or were captured. A few survived by gnawing flesh cut from still-living horses or the bodies of their dead comrades.

POISONED!

After his final defeat in 1815, Napoleon was exiled to the island of St Helena. He died in 1821. At the time it was thought he died of cancer, but forensic tests have since revealed that his body contained large amounts of arsenic, possibly from his hair oil, from inhaling wallpaper fumes, or most likely from the hand of an assassin. The chief suspect is Charles Tristan, marquis de Montholon.

DEATH RITUALS

Funerals and cremations may involve strange rituals or unusual coffins and in the past, they included some cruel ceremonies.

In Tibet, one Buddhist ritual involves cutting up the body of someone who has died and laying out the pieces for vultures to peck at.

FANTASY FUNERALS

Fancy coffins have become a feature of funerals in parts of the West African country of Ghana. A carpenter will build you a coffin to look like a jet plane, an elephant, an eagle, a fish, a racing car or even a giant mobile phone. What a way to impress your friends when you go!

AMAZING!

ROYAL SACRIFICE

In ancient times, in parts of Europe and Asia, it was common for the servants and slaves of kings and queens to be sacrificed at a royal funeral, so that they could serve their rulers in the next world. The Great Death Pit at Ur, in ancient Iraq, contained 70 bodies.

Early in his reign, the Egyptian pharaoh Ramesses II started building a splendid memorial temple to himself, where people could worship him after his death.

MUMMIES

Dead bodies are sometimes specially preserved by drying, so that they do not rot. They are made into mummies, like the Egyptian one below. The earliest intact human mummy from Egypt dates back to 3400 BC. Even older deliberately mummified bodies have been found in South America. The Chinchorro mummies from northern Chile date from about 5050 BC.

CRUEL FLAMES

In the past, in India, wives would sometimes throw themselves on the fire when their husbands were cremated (they left their handprints before they went to their fiery death). This was called sati. The aim was to show how devoted they were. Sometimes they were forced to do it. Occasionally, sati has happened in modern times, but strict laws now ban this cruel practice.

IN LOVING MEMORY

We may remember the dead with sadness or with respect, or because those who died chose bizarre ways to remind us of their lives.

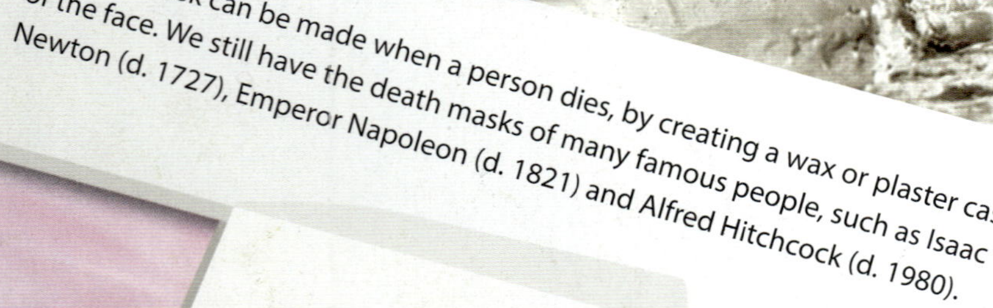

A death mask can be made when a person dies, by creating a wax or plaster cast of the face. We still have the death masks of many famous people, such as Isaac Newton (d. 1727), Emperor Napoleon (d. 1821) and Alfred Hitchcock (d. 1980).

DIAMONDS ARE FOREVER

Modern jewellers use carbon extracted from the ashes of the cremated body of a loved one, or from their hair, to make a diamond. This can be worn on a ring, at a cost of up to £16,000!

BURIED UPSIDE DOWN

A memorial stone on Box Hill, near Dorking in England, marks the burial place of Major Peter Labelliere. He died in 1800 and was buried standing on his head. He had read that the world would be turned upside down on Judgement Day and believed that when that day came, he would be the only person left standing the right way up!

KEPT ON SHOW

English eccentric Jeremy Bentham arranged for his body to be displayed after his death in 1832. His head was mummified and his skeleton was padded out with straw and dressed in his clothes. Later, a wax head was made. Since 1850, Jeremy has been on public display at University College, London. Sometimes he even attends meetings of the College, but they won't let him vote!

ROSEMARY

Throughout history, the herb rosemary has been linked with remembering the dead. It was strewn in graveyards so that its scent would mask the smell of rotting corpses. Some people came to believe that rosemary could preserve bodies. A sprig placed in the hands of a dead person would sometimes take root in the human remains and push upwards, breaking open the vault.

Monsters, vampires, skeletons and devils make fun costumes at Halloween, but at one time, masks and costumes really were designed to scare the living daylights out of anyone who saw them.

WITCH DOCTORS

Before medicines became widely available, many cultures around the world had witch doctors. It was believed that these wise men or women could interact with the spirit world to protect people from witchcraft. They also used herbal medicine to assist with childbirth, tooth extraction and illness. If their remedies failed, they commonly blamed the failure on the displeasure of the gods.

MASKS AND MAGIC

Africa is famous for its masks, made to be worn in dances, entertainments, funerals or secret ceremonies. Some were masks of animals or people, some of spirits or ghosts. All were believed to have magical powers. Some masks were beautiful, but others were hideous, designed to chill the blood and horrify.

DAY OF THE DEAD

Dressed-up skeleton dolls, skull-shaped sweets and parades of revellers in skeleton costumes. Welcome to Mexico's Day of the Dead, celebrated each year at the beginning of November. Morbid and miserable? Not at all! This ancient festival is all about honouring and celebrating the lives of the dead. Deceased children are remembered on 1st November (All Saints Day) and adults on 2nd November (All Souls Day).

For the Day of the Dead festival, people set up an altar in their house and cover it with 'offerings' for the deceased. The most popular are sugar skulls, elaborately decorated with icing, feathers and sequins.

HEAD SHRINKERS

Long ago, the Shuar and Achuar warriors of the South American rainforest would cut off the heads of their enemies. They removed the skull and brain, boiled the remains, cut away the flesh and dried the skin with hot sand. Why did they shrink the heads? To win control of the dead man's spirit. Sometimes the heads were worn on cords around the neck.

DEVIL MASKS

For Fastnacht, a carnival held before Lent in southern Germany, Switzerland and Austria, people wear scary carnival masks that look like devils with twisted faces. These represent the dark spirits of winter, which must be hunted down and expelled before Spring can come and life can start again.

BEASTLY BEAUTY

People will go to extraordinary lengths to 'look good'. Over the ages, they have done some gruesome things to themselves in the name of beauty.

BIG WIGS

In the 1770s, the most fashionable ladies of Paris and London wore towering wigs and hairpieces. These were built around horsehair pads and were held together with pins, wire, ribbons, powder and a kind of grease called pomade. If the wigs weren't looked after properly, they soon attracted vermin and even, so they say, nesting mice!

FAT AS THAT... OR THIN AS A PIN?

In the 1860s the beautiful wives of King Rumanika of Karagwe, in Africa, were forced to drink milk all day long until they became as fat as seals and could no longer stand upright. At the same time in Europe, incredibly narrow waists were in fashion. Ladies wore corsets that were laced so tightly that they deformed the body and damaged the ribs, heart and lungs.

AMAZING!

LIQUID FAT

Today, over 400,000 people a year in the United States have liposuction to remove bulges from their bodies and re-shape themselves. A tube is inserted under the skin, most commonly on the thighs, buttocks, neck, upper arms and calves, then the fat there is broken down and sucked out by the jugful. How gross!

DID YOU KNOW?

GRUESOME GAP-FILLERS

False teeth were originally made from second-hand human or animal teeth. US President George Washington's fine set of false choppers was made out of hippopotamus tusk.

BAD MAKE-UP DAY

In the days of the Roman Empire, a woman might have used cosmetics made of onions in chicken fat, crushed beetles, animal urine, soot, vinegar, asses' milk, sulphur, or as a very special treat, expensively imported crocodile dung. So what is in modern make-up? You'll need an advanced knowledge of chemistry to understand the ingredients!

TOOTH WHITENERS

People have always wanted gleaming teeth. Before good dentists came along, all sorts of toothpastes and mouthwashes were invented and some of them were pretty gruesome! How would you fancy brushing with tortoise blood, burnt mouse heads, stale urine, charcoal or cuttlefish bone?

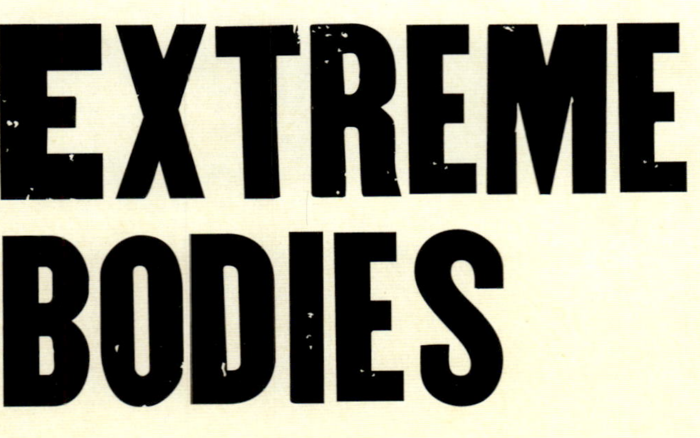

EXTREME BODIES

Huge lip plates, painted skin, body piercings and neck rings. Humans have deformed and mistreated their bodies in the strangest ways over the ages.

BODY PIERCING

For more than 5,000 years, people have been piercing their bodies. Sometimes they do it for religious reasons, but often it's just a form of self-expression. A few people go wild and have hundreds, or even thousands, of piercings. The world record holder claimed, in 2012, to have 9,000!

NICE PLATE!

The Mursi or Mun people live in an isolated part of southwestern Ethiopia, in Africa. Traditionally, they paint their bodies with sacred clays and the women wear large clay 'plates' in their lower lips, used to serve food to their husband. Increasingly, the plates are also worn as a way of earning extra money from tourists.

STARS IN YOUR EYES

In 2004, a Dutch surgeon invented eyeball jewellery. The membrane or layer covering the eye is sliced open and a tiny heart, moon or star made of platinum is inserted directly into the eye. At first this feels a bit gritty, but the eye heals up after a week or so. Eye experts in Britain and the USA were quick to warn that this operation could be very dangerous.

Tattooing is an ancient art dating back over 5,000 years, but some people take it to extremes and cover their entire body, and even the inside of their mouth and ears, with tattoos.

BRASS COILS

The Kayan Lawhi or Padaung women of Burma (Myanmar) traditionally wear brass coils around their necks to make them look longer. More and more coils are added over the years. The neck does not actually grow longer, but the bones of the body are pushed down and deformed. The custom has been criticised in Burma (Myanmar) and many women have removed the coils. However, some Kayan refugees living in Thailand have been paid to continue this custom in order to attract tourists.

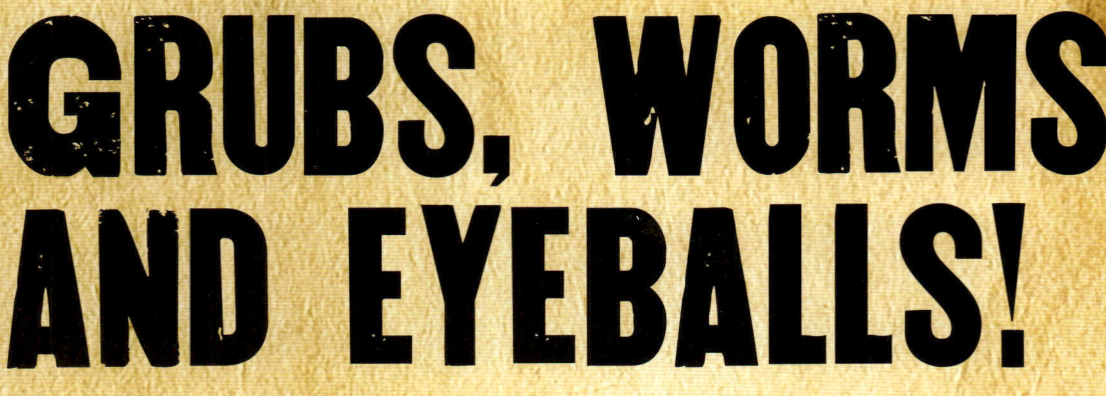

GRUBS, WORMS AND EYEBALLS!

These bizarre titbits may look disgusting to you, but to someone else they are tasty treats filled with goodness, and they're delicious, too!

TUCK IN!

People in Southeast Asia don't let any food go to waste, that's why food stalls often sell a delicious chicken or duck combo kebab of roasted hearts, feet and tails. Chicken gizzards (stomachs) are a popular traditional food in China.

GOURMET GRUBS

They are large, squashy, juicy, tasty and really good for you, so why not tuck into a nice fat grub? Witchetty grubs come from Australia and are the larvae (caterpillars) of moths. They taste a bit like scrambled eggs and can be eaten raw or lightly cooked.

AMAZING!

SWEET SNACK

Silk worms are the larvae of moths and they are used to make silk. In Burma (Myanmar), they are deep-fried until they puff up like corn snacks and are served with a lovely coating of honey.

DID YOU KNOW?

FRUIT BAT SOUP

In the islands around Thailand, a whole fruit bat is dunked live into a simmering pot to make a popular soup. Herbs, spices and coconut milk are added, but they can't take away the nasty taste of bat. These flying mammals also carry diseases, so this is not a recipe we recommend.

If someone offers you a sheep's eye, remember to pop it into your mouth whole. Then crunch it up to enjoy the slimy liquid pouring out, it's a delicacy in parts of Arabia and Africa.

FREAKY FOOD HERO

William Buckland (1784–1856) was a freaky food hero. His ambition was to eat an example of every animal that lived, from puppies to panthers. He even tried bats' wee. His most loved dish was mice on toast, but he wasn't keen on insects, especially bluebottles and earwigs.

You can eat mealworms (baby beetles) raw, but the best way is to dry roast them, just like peanuts. Then you can add them to muffins, yum!

FREAKY FOODS

If you like trying new foods, you need to travel. These dishes are loved by nations around the world.

HOPPY MEAL

There are millions more kangaroos in Australia than there are humans. In fact, there are so many roos jumping about that eating them is one way to control their numbers. Kangaroo meat is also very healthy, because it's full of protein and has less fat than other meats.

PIG TAILS

The French are famous for their wonderful cooking skills, so it's no wonder they can make pigs' heads and tails taste good. The tails need to be cooked slowly to get the best taste, but nibbling on the skinny, bony bits is still hard work and not as good as barbecue spare ribs!

ANT CROUTONS

Ants are added to salads in Venezuela. They are deep-fried and then sprinkled over the top to add a slightly smoky taste and a crunch!

AMAZING!

FURRY FRIENDS

We think of guinea pigs as pets, but in Peru people think of these little furry animals as… lunch! They are bred on guinea-pig farms. People often cook them over an open flame and serve them up on a bed of lettuce.

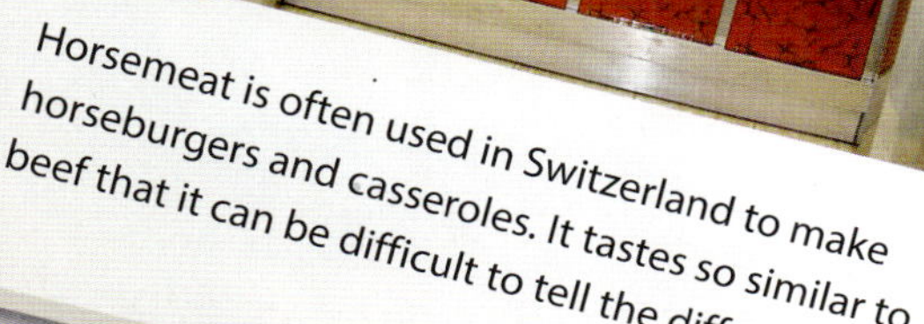

Horsemeat is often used in Switzerland to make horseburgers and casseroles. It tastes so similar to beef that it can be difficult to tell the difference.

TERMITE TREAT

Children in Uganda can't get their hands on sweets and chocolate very easily, but they can enjoy a healthier treat, termites! These ant-like insects are caught in their flying season. Their wings are removed and then they are boiled and fried.

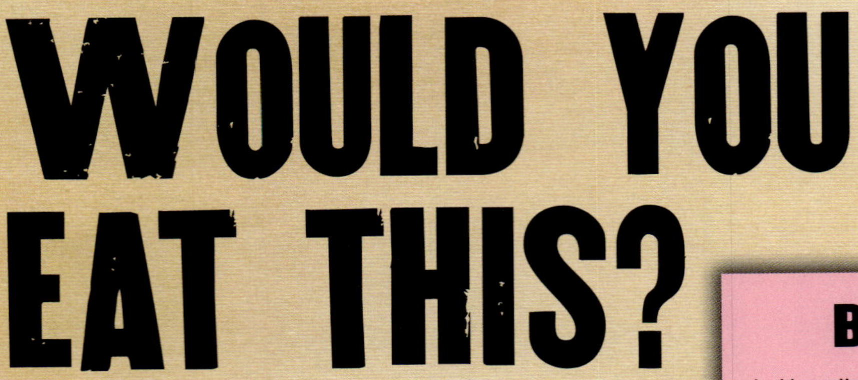

WOULD YOU EAT THIS?

Do you believe that a dog is man's best friend? Or do you think there's nothing better than dog stew? What's not acceptable in one country may be perfectly okay somewhere else!

BARKING MAD

In Hawaii, puppies are cooked over a bed of burning coals and served with a dish of sweet potatoes. Long ago, Mexican hairless dogs were bred to be eaten and were the Aztecs' main meat. Dogs have been eaten in Korea for more than 6,000 years and dog dishes are still popular there today.

ANYONE FOR UDDER?

Udders are the part of a cow where milk is made and where calves suck to get at the milk. It's hard to believe, but for centuries they were a popular type of meat in England and France. Udders were boiled and added to stews, or cooked and sliced as cold meat, like ham.

GOAT BURGER

Hot, dry countries are not always the best place to rear cattle, which need lots of green grass to thrive. Instead, people rear goats and turn their meat into burgers, pies or stews. Donkeys, mules and water buffalo are also likely to be on the menu.

A single swarm of locusts can contain many millions of flying insects and as they travel they eat every plant in their path. What better way to get your own back than to tuck into a plateful of boiled locusts?

WARNING!

CHOKING HAZARD

If you fancy eating grasshoppers or locusts, it's a good idea to remove their long, spindly hind legs first. Although the legs have got some delicious meat in them, they are also covered in small spines and can get caught in your throat, just like fish bones.

FRIED FEET

Bears used to live in the forests of Europe and were often hunted for food. A very popular treat in several countries was a dish of bears' paws. They were coated in breadcrumbs and fried in butter or oil, just like chicken nuggets!

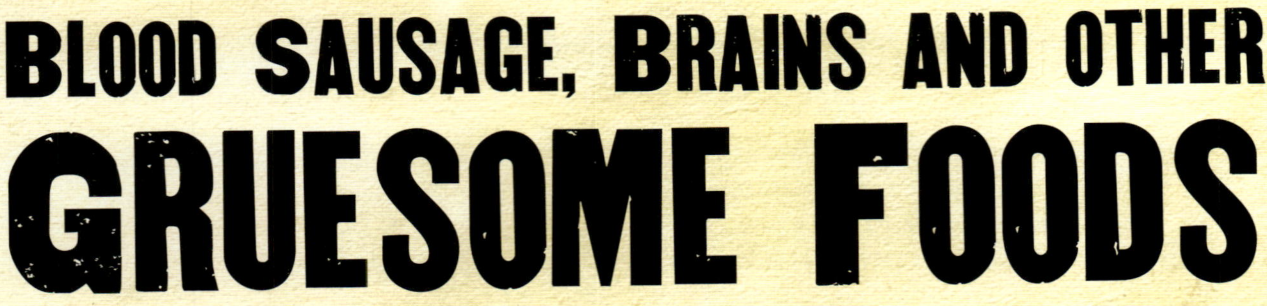

BLOOD SAUSAGE, BRAINS AND OTHER GRUESOME FOODS

Would you eat something if you could see its face looking back at you? Eating heads and brains is weird!

HEAD CHEESE

Head cheese isn't made of cheese, but the bad news is that it's definitely made of heads! Usually pigs' or calves' heads are used. Chefs are told to remove the eyes and skin and to clear the ear canals of wax, how gross! The meat is then boiled and a pig's foot may be added for more taste.

HEADS UP

If you had to cook a calf's head, a popular dish in France known as 'tête de veau', where would you begin? You'd remove all the fur and skin first. Next, you'd cut it in half, roll it around a calf's tongue and cook it in a big pan with water and seasoning for about five hours. Now serve it cut into slices, with a bit of brain on top. How gross is that?

Blood sausages are popular around the world and in England they are part of a fried breakfast. They are called black pudding and are made from pigs' blood.

MIND OVER MATTER

Brains are soft, squishy and spongy, so eating them is more like eating a grainy jelly than eating other types of meat. They are enjoyed all over the world and are served in many different ways, from boiling to frying. In some places, brains are spread on toast with salt and in Austria pig brains are cooked into scrambled egg.

FAT FURTERS

Lots of people love to eat the pale pink sausages called frankfurters, but would you still eat one if you knew what went into it? Cheap frankfurters are made from a meat paste made in a factory from leftover bits of pig. The paste is then mashed with fake tastes and shades and extra water and salt are added.

HAVE SOME MORE?

Are you someone who's always ready for second helpings? You might not be so keen on some of these lovely dishes.

SLIMY STARTERS

Collecting and selling mopani worms is big business in southern Africa. These grubs are caterpillars that live on trees and they are served up in homes and restaurants. Before they are eaten, the caterpillars are squeezed until their green, slimy insides slide out.

11A

11A

DEAD AND RED

Did you know that some red food dye, such as the kind used to dye icing, gets its shade from dead insects called cochineals? They live on cactuses and have to be collected by hand to be turned into a natural dye. Cochineal dye is also added to meats to make them look fresh.

COFFEE SURPRISE

You could finish your gruesome meal with a delightful cup of kopi luwak coffee. It is made from coffee beans that have been eaten and pooed out by wild civets (cat-like animals). It has a slight taste of chocolate...

This is probably the most disgusting cheese in the world! It is called *casu marzu* and is full of wriggling, munching maggots that break down the cheese's fats.

DID YOU KNOW?

KILLER BEANS

Dried kidney beans look harmless, but they can make you extremely ill if they are not properly prepared. The beans make a poison to stop insects from eating them, but it can make humans sick, too. The poison can be destroyed by soaking the beans for 12 hours and then cooking them. Luckily, canned kidney beans are completely safe.

PRESERVING BODIES

Left alone, a dead body decomposes or rots, but there are a number of ways to preserve bodies.

HOLY RELICS

In the Middle Ages, churches and kings kept bones, skulls, fingers and other body parts of saints as holy relics. King Louis IX (St Louis) of France collected all kinds of Christian relics. When, in 1270, he died in North Africa, his own bones were boiled until all the flesh was gone, so they could be taken back to France.

AMAZING!

PICKLED IN BRANDY

Admiral Nelson's victory at the Battle of Trafalgar, in 1805, was met with both celebration and sadness. The threat to England of invasion by Napoleon had been removed, but Nelson was dead. Onboard his ship, his body was placed in a large barrel filled with brandy to preserve it, while it was sailed back to England. It was then put in a brandy-filled lead coffin while the state funeral was arranged. Alcohol preserved his body for over two months (October 21, 1805-January 9, 1806).

Suicide was often a ritual, performed in a special way. To avoid dishonour, a Japanese nobleman would slash his stomach open with his samurai sword.

EMBALMING

Undertakers embalm bodies for funerals, replacing blood in the veins with chemicals. They make the body look as lifelike as possible, even sewing up the lips to keep the mouth shut. Sometimes embalmed bodies are put on public display. The North Korean leader Kim Il Sung (d. 1994) lies in a glass case inside a palace.

RIGOR MORTIS

Rigor mortis is the stiffening of a body after death. It starts 3-4 hours after a person has died. Within 12 hours a body may be completely rigid, although it stiffens more quickly in a warm room. Rigor wears off within 2-2½ days.

MODERN MUMMIFICATION

Long ago, the Egyptians mummified bodies to preserve them. They removed the insides, sucking out the brain through the nose, then dried and padded the corpse and wrapped it in cloth. Today, a different method is used. Bodies (including those of pet cats) are submerged in preservation fluid for several months. It's claimed that this way, the body's DNA is preserved, so the individual could one day be cloned back to life.

BODY WORLDS

The first anatomists had to work fast to dissect bodies before they decomposed. Now, science has found ways to keep bodies lifelike forever.

BOTTLED!

From the late 1800s, scientists used chemicals such as formaldehyde to kill bacteria and preserve human and animal remains. Museums kept pickled fish, reptiles and other animals, while medical schools kept human body parts. Although formaldehyde slows down decay, it cannot preserve a body forever.

PLASTIC PEOPLE

Plastination is a technique invented in the 1970s by German anatomist Gunther von Hagens. Basically, he invented a way to make long-lasting plastic bodies. Plastination works by replacing water and fat in a dead body with plastics called polymer resins. The plastics preserve the body so that it does not smell and can be handled by students or posed to look lifelike.

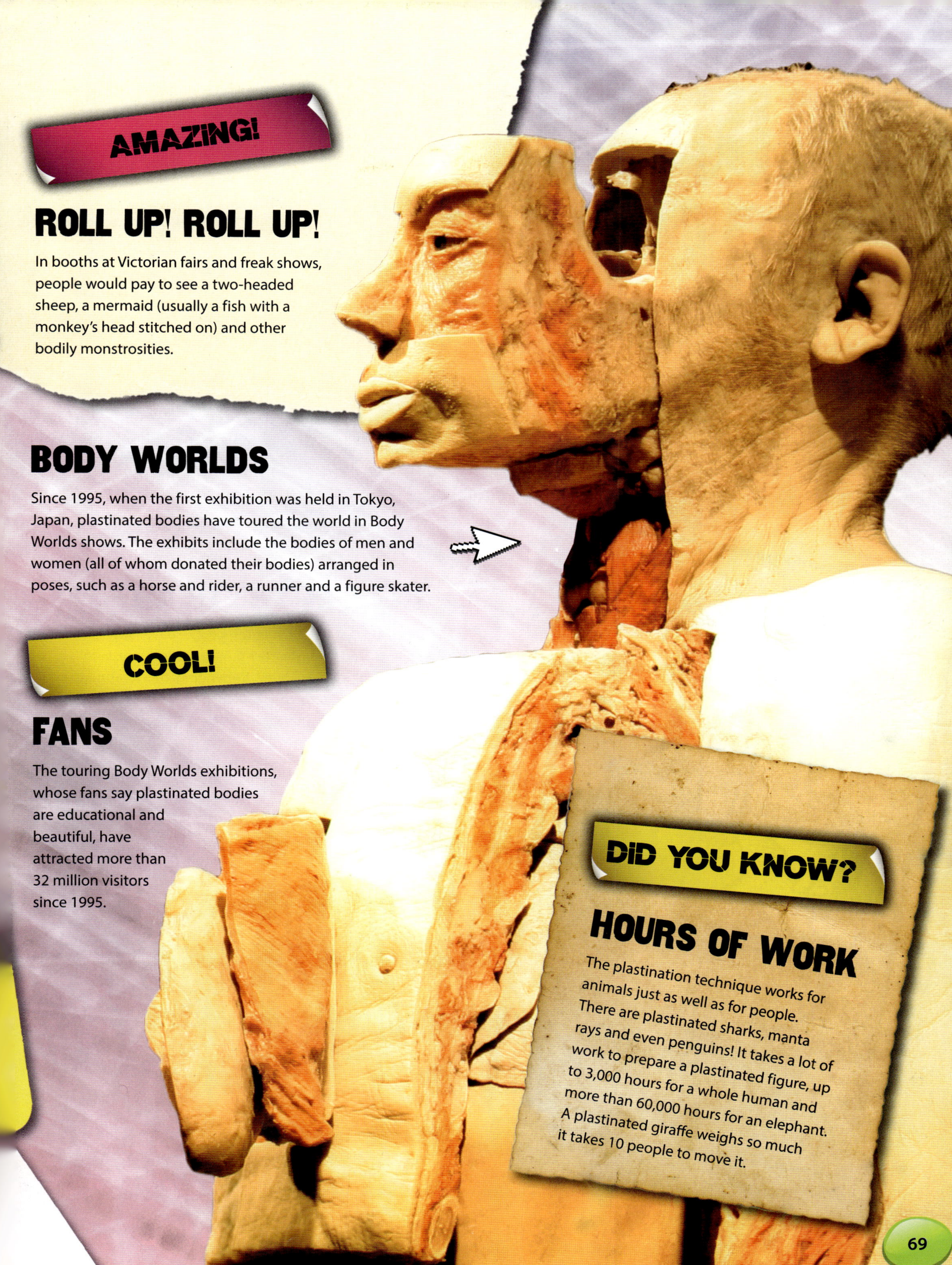

AMAZING!

ROLL UP! ROLL UP!

In booths at Victorian fairs and freak shows, people would pay to see a two-headed sheep, a mermaid (usually a fish with a monkey's head stitched on) and other bodily monstrosities.

BODY WORLDS

Since 1995, when the first exhibition was held in Tokyo, Japan, plastinated bodies have toured the world in Body Worlds shows. The exhibits include the bodies of men and women (all of whom donated their bodies) arranged in poses, such as a horse and rider, a runner and a figure skater.

COOL!

FANS

The touring Body Worlds exhibitions, whose fans say plastinated bodies are educational and beautiful, have attracted more than 32 million visitors since 1995.

DID YOU KNOW?

HOURS OF WORK

The plastination technique works for animals just as well as for people. There are plastinated sharks, manta rays and even penguins! It takes a lot of work to prepare a plastinated figure, up to 3,000 hours for a whole human and more than 60,000 hours for an elephant. A plastinated giraffe weighs so much it takes 10 people to move it.

PAIN AND MORE PAIN

Until the 1800s, surgery was painful and dangerous. There were no painkillers or drugs and there was lots of dirt and infection.

BLIND EGYPTIANS!

Curious cures were common in ancient times. To treat blindness, ancient Egyptians mashed up pigs' eyes, added honey and red ochre (an earthy pigment containing ferric oxide) and then poured the mixture into the patient's ear!

HOLE IN THE HEAD

Since ancient Egyptian times, people have had holes drilled through their skulls to relieve pressure beneath the bone. Called 'trepanning', this treatment was believed to cure fits and madness. The ancient Egyptians did it without anaesthetics, yikes!

Wounded soldiers from the Crimean War (1850s) ended up in filthy hospitals full of rats, until nurse Florence Nightingale came along and revolutionized nursing.

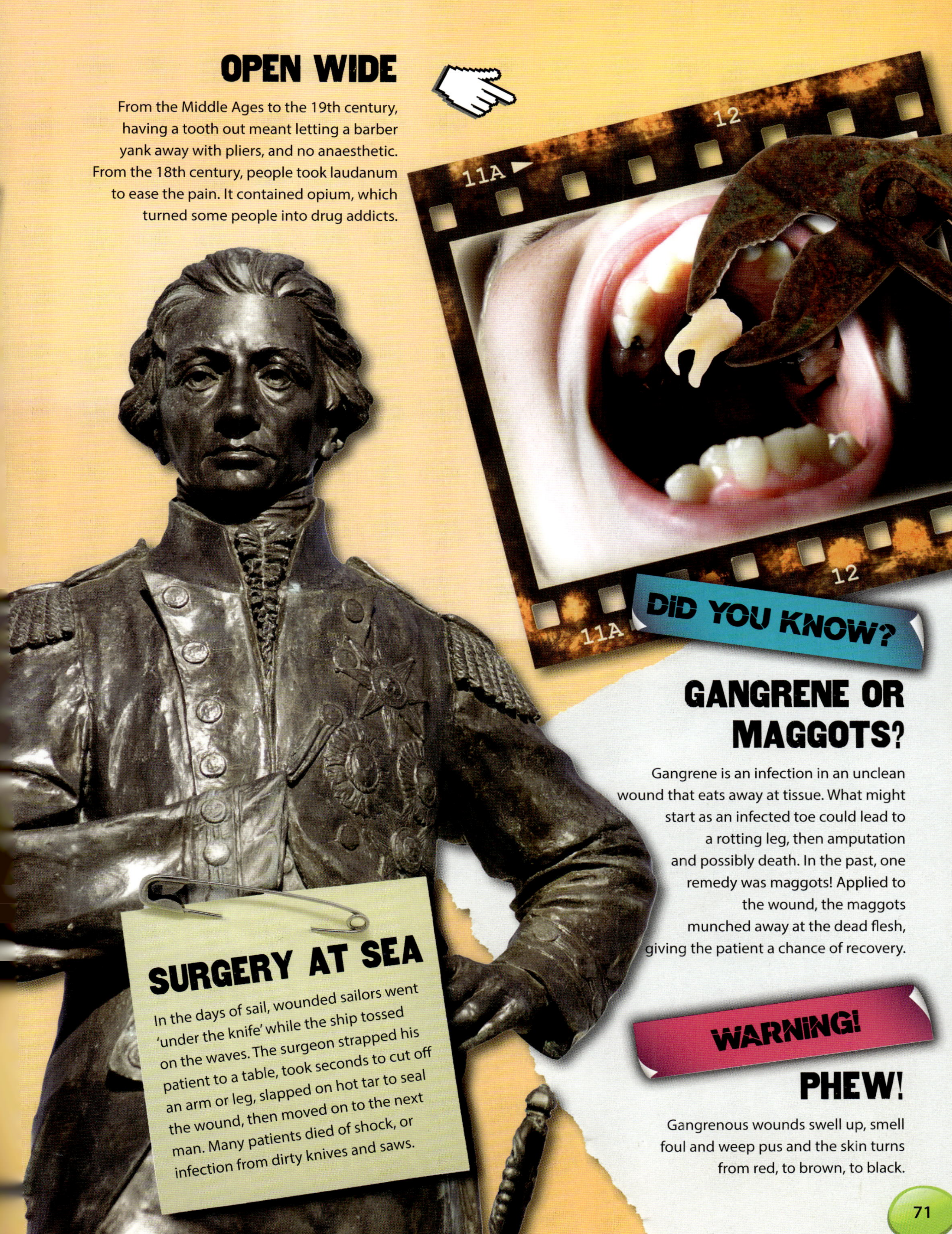

OPEN WIDE

From the Middle Ages to the 19th century, having a tooth out meant letting a barber yank away with pliers, and no anaesthetic. From the 18th century, people took laudanum to ease the pain. It contained opium, which turned some people into drug addicts.

SURGERY AT SEA

In the days of sail, wounded sailors went 'under the knife' while the ship tossed on the waves. The surgeon strapped his patient to a table, took seconds to cut off an arm or leg, slapped on hot tar to seal the wound, then moved on to the next man. Many patients died of shock, or infection from dirty knives and saws.

DID YOU KNOW?

GANGRENE OR MAGGOTS?

Gangrene is an infection in an unclean wound that eats away at tissue. What might start as an infected toe could lead to a rotting leg, then amputation and possibly death. In the past, one remedy was maggots! Applied to the wound, the maggots munched away at the dead flesh, giving the patient a chance of recovery.

WARNING!

PHEW!

Gangrenous wounds swell up, smell foul and weep pus and the skin turns from red, to brown, to black.

BODY SNATCHERS

Doctors learn about the body by cutting it open, but for many years, practical anatomy was against the law. To get a body, a doctor had to pay a body snatcher.

RAISING THE DEAD

Before 1832, when a law was passed allowing more bodies to be used for medical dissection, only the corpses of hanged murderers were available to medical students. Sometimes doctors turned to grave robbers, known as 'resurrection men' because they 'raised the dead' to supply them with bodies.

DID YOU KNOW?

AGAINST THE LAW

Throughout Medieval Europe and the early Renaissance, the Catholic Church prohibited the mutilation (cutting up) of Christian bodies and civil laws forbade the dissection of corpses in general.

SCALPELS OUT

Andreas Vesalius (1514–64) revolutionized the study of human anatomy. He broke with Medieval tradition by personally cutting up corpses (executed criminals) in front of his students and challenging the centuries-old teachings of Galen that were normally taught to anatomy students. At Padua University, his students had to work in secret, in rooms with no windows, so the smell wouldn't alert the authorities. During the 17th century, the public would sometimes pay to watch anatomy lessons, as here at the University of Leiden, Holland.

DID YOU KNOW?

MORTSAFES

Rich families locked up their dead inside stone vaults, which were fairly secure. Ordinary graves were more at risk from theft. From 1816, people could buy an iron grid or box, called a 'mortsafe', to put over a grave, so that robbers couldn't force off the gravestone and steal the body inside.

BURKE AND HARE

In Scotland, in the early 1800s, two body snatchers named William Burke and William Hare sold corpses to an Edinburgh doctor, Robert Knox. When demand exceeded supply, the pair turned to murder and killed 16 people. Later, Hare put the blame on Burke, who was hanged in 1829. The expression 'to burke' meant to strangle someone, leaving no sign of violence.

TUNNEL ROBBERS

To guard against body-theft, which became increasingly common, cemetery guardians were posted to keep watch from specially built towers. Some grave robbers dug tunnels to get into graves, looping a rope around the corpse to pull it out.

BEAUTY TREATMENTS

In pursuit of beauty, people don't always stop to consider the medical consequences. Beauty treatments can be painful and even fatal.

AMAZING!

PLUCK IT OUT

In Europe in the 1400s to 1500s, fashion-conscious women plucked not only their eyebrows, but also all the hair from the front of their heads. The idea was to make the hairline recede and the forehead look bigger, ouch!

Plunging your feet into a fish spa bath feels pretty weird. As the 'doctor fish' nibble away at the feet looking for food, they dislodge little bits of old, dead skin. Some US states have banned fish spas, fearing they could spread infections.

THE BIG SQUEEZE

One way that many people tackle obesity is to have a gastric band fitted to their stomach to slow down eating and reduce their appetite. Although often successful, complications can occur. The band can slip, bulge through the skin, or cause blood clots. Successful weight loss also leaves a person with baggy sacs of loose, wrinkly skin. Lovely!

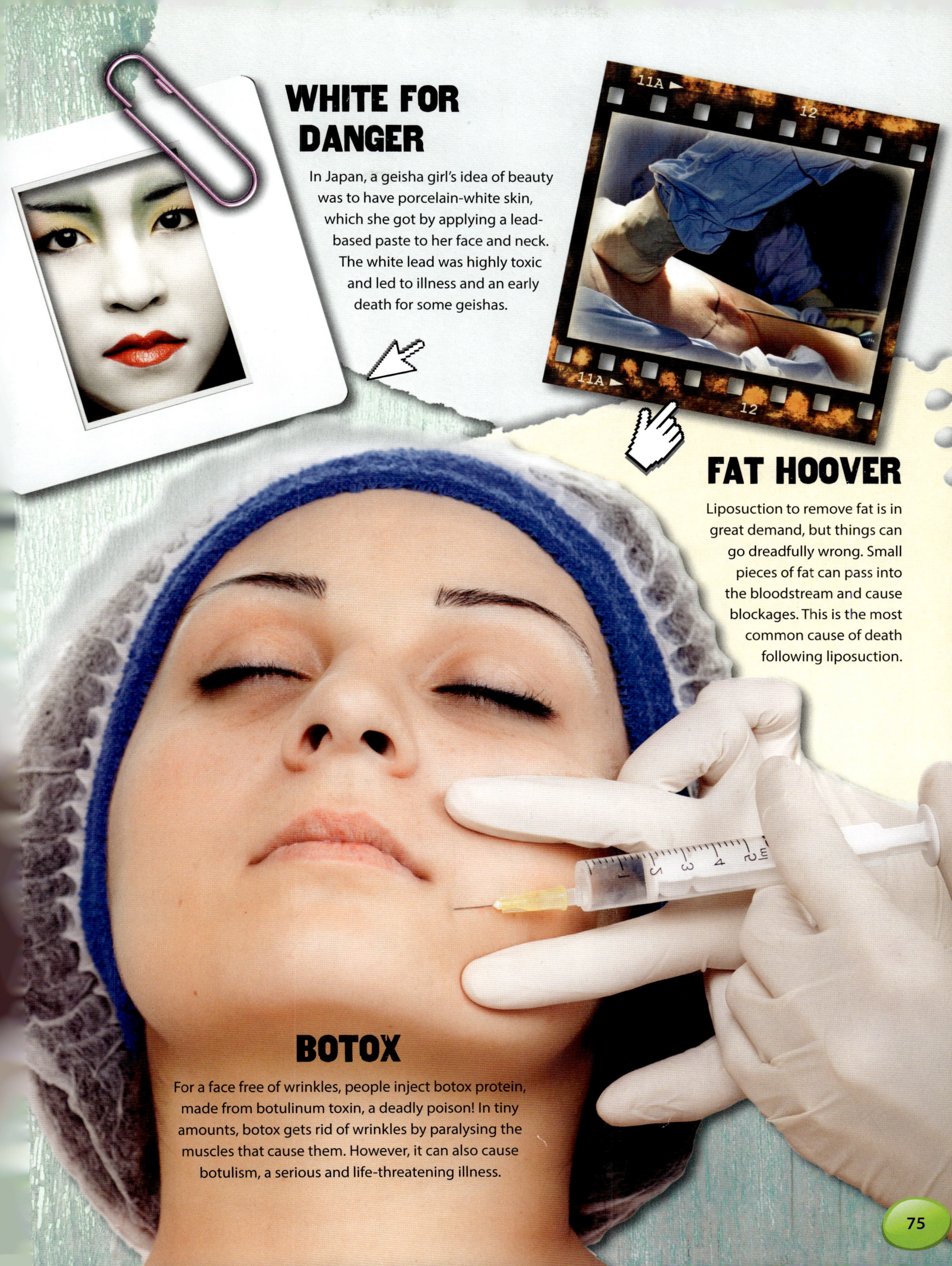

WHITE FOR DANGER

In Japan, a geisha girl's idea of beauty was to have porcelain-white skin, which she got by applying a lead-based paste to her face and neck. The white lead was highly toxic and led to illness and an early death for some geishas.

FAT HOOVER

Liposuction to remove fat is in great demand, but things can go dreadfully wrong. Small pieces of fat can pass into the bloodstream and cause blockages. This is the most common cause of death following liposuction.

BOTOX

For a face free of wrinkles, people inject botox protein, made from botulinum toxin, a deadly poison! In tiny amounts, botox gets rid of wrinkles by paralysing the muscles that cause them. However, it can also cause botulism, a serious and life-threatening illness.

QUAKES AND WAVES

Is the ground beneath us solid and safe? No! The planet's crust quakes and shakes. Earthquakes can destroy great cities and also trigger terrifying walls of water, called tsunamis.

WHY THE BIG SHAKE UP?

The rocks that make up the Earth's surface are a bit like an eggshell cracked into about 20 sections, called plates. These float on a layer of gooey rock, called 'mantle'. The edges of the plates often bump, grind and crunch together, with a force powerful enough to push up the world's biggest mountain ranges.

TERROR QUAKES

Just before an earthquake happens, the world suddenly falls silent. Even the dogs stop barking. Suddenly there is a great rumble or roar. Highways crack open, bridges fall into rivers and apartment blocks collapse into rubble. Homes are crushed like cardboard. Gas pipes catch fire and water mains burst open. Such is the terror of a major earthquake.

AMAZING!

WORST EVER

The 1556 earthquake in Shaanxi, China, had the worst death toll of any earthquake in history. It killed about 830,000 people.

BIGGEST EVER

The biggest-ever earthquake struck Valdivia, Chile, in 1960, with a magnitude of 9.5.

WALLS OF WATER

An earthquake below the ocean floor can trigger a massive shock. The pressure sends a mighty whoosh of water racing through the ocean. As it approaches the coast, this is raised into a giant wave. The sea drains back from beaches and then a wall of water rushes in. The Japanese tsunami of 2011 towered to a height of 40.4 m (133 ft) and in places smashed its way 10 km (6 miles) inland. It killed 15,883 people and caused disastrous accidents at nuclear power plants.

HAITI'S HORROR

When a magnitude 7.0 earthquake struck Haiti in 2010, its people lost everything. At least 220,000 people were killed, over 300,000 were injured and 1.5 million were made homeless. More than 293,000 houses and 4,000 schools were badly damaged or destroyed and the capital, Port-au-Prince, was engulfed in tonnes of rubble.

VOLCANO!

Long ago, people thought that the sulphurous, glowing craters of volcanoes were the gateways to hell. We still fear these mountains of fire today, with good reason!

TEMPTING FATE

The green slopes of a tropical volcano might seem to be the ideal place to start a farm. The soil is black, crumbly and very fertile. Who knows, the volcano might not erupt for hundreds of years, but what if you are unlucky? When a volcano blows its top, it can rip the whole mountainside apart. You may be poisoned by deadly gas, bombed by rocks, choked by ash, swallowed up by molten rock or burnt alive.

RING OF FIRE

The rim of the Pacific Ocean is often called the Ring of Fire. The geology there is restless along a vast arc that takes in New Zealand, Southeast Asia, Japan, Russia and North and South America. This 'ring' has 452 volcanoes and a high risk of spectacular earthquakes and tsunamis. Welcome to the ultimate danger zone!

BURIED ALIVE

When Italy's Mount Vesuvius erupted in 79 AD, the port of Herculaneum was engulfed by a torrent of boiling mud 13 m (42 ft) deep. Archaeologists have found the skeletons of victims who were trying to escape by boat. The inland town of Pompeii was buried under ash, in places 3.5 m (11.5 ft) deep. Where corpses were buried, their bodies left cavities in the ash. By filling these spaces with plaster, archaeologists have been able to recreate the likeness of the victims at the moment they died.

COOL FACT!

BIG BANG

The 1883 explosion of Krakatoa, a volcanic island in Indonesia, is said to have been heard about 3,000 miles (4,800 km) away. The eruption spewed ash 50 miles (80 km) into space. The death toll was somewhere between 36,000 and 120,000.

LAVA

Under the Earth's crust, Earth is made of hot, liquid rock, called magma. When this liquid rock erupts out of a volcano, it's called lava. The lava flows in red-hot rivers down the side of the volcano and hardens as it cools. Cooled lava has formed many mountains and island chains.

ROLLING DEATH

A pyroclastic flow is a wall of smoke, gases and ash that can be as hot as 1,000°C (1,830°F). It can roll down a mountainside at over 250 kmph (155 mph). In 1902, a deadly pyroclastic flow from Mt Pelée in Martinique killed about 30,000 people in the town of Saint-Pierre.

ROARING AVALANCHES

An avalanche gathers up snow, ice, soil, rocks and trees as it goes, until it weighs hundreds of thousands of tonnes. Anything in its path, people, houses, villages or vehicles, will be swept away. Better watch out!

WHITE DEATH

Snow can be wet, powdery, loose or closely bound. Any one of these can be fatal when hurtling down a mountain. An avalanche can be triggered naturally, when a mass of snow starts to break up during a thaw or storm, but skiing or using snowmobiles may also set one off.

BURIED ALIVE

If you are buried alive under an avalanche, you may have about 18 minutes to live before you suffocate. Your limbs may be broken, or you may die of hypothermia. The most important piece of equipment to carry is a beacon or transceiver, which sends out location signals to others on the mountain.

DID YOU KNOW?

"AVALANCHE!"

Sometimes mountain rangers set off avalanches on purpose, with explosives. These are controlled exercises to relieve the build-up of snow on the peak at a time when all is clear below.

SERIAL KILLER

Mount Huascarán in Peru is the world's cruellest mountain. In 1962, an avalanche of ice and rock buried whole towns and villages, killing 4,000 people. In 1970, an earthquake set off another wall of ice, rock and snow that hurtled for 16 km (10 miles) at speeds of up to 280 kmph (174 mph). This time the death toll was 20,000.

AMAZING!

AVALANCHE EXPRESS

In 1910, the Spokane Express, a train bound for Seattle in the United States, got trapped in a blizzard and snow drifts at Wellington station for five days. Then an avalanche rumbled down Windy Mountain. It slammed into the express and a mail train. The carriages were swept into a deep gorge and 96 passengers and crew were killed.

NO ESCAPE!

We all have a deep-rooted fear of being dragged down into something that we can't escape from. If you get sucked into a bog, swamp, quicksand or a whirlpool, the chances of rescue are slim. What a gruesome way to go!

BOG TERRORS

Bogs and marshes are scary places. Venture off the path and you may find yourself squelching and flailing as you sink into the slime. The bogs of Europe contain dead people that are thousands of years old. Their bodies are often found, perfectly preserved, in these cold, acidic, oxygen-free environments. Many seem to be Iron Age human sacrifices or executed prisoners.

SWAMP KILLER

The real danger from swamps is not so much the terrain as the creatures that live there. The deadliest of all is the mosquito. This insect breeds in wetlands and some species pass on malaria, a disease that kills between 584,000 and 2.7 million people worldwide each year. That really is a natural disaster.

WHIRLING WATERS

Whirlpool, vortex, maelstrom... All these words describe the spot where powerful tides and currents collide, creating a deadly, spinning wheel of water in seas and straits. Whirlpool currents can reach 37 kmph (23 mph), as around the Moskstraumen eddies in the Norwegian Sea. Fishermen and kayakers must be careful if they want to avoid being pulled down to drown in the seaweed.

AMAZING!

HELP!

Swampy environments make rescue or salvage extremely difficult. In 1996, a DC-9 passenger jet crashed into a deep-water swamp in Florida, with the loss of 110 lives. Access to the crash was extremely hazardous because of the thick vegetation and the alligators!

QUICKSAND PANIC

When sand is saturated with water, the pressure from one step can turn it into a quivering jelly, called quicksand.
If someone sinks in, the more they thrash around, the worse it gets. If it happens to you, here's what to do. Spread out you arms and legs very slowly and try to get on your back. You'll float safely more often than the horror movies let on!
The real danger is panic, and of course the incoming tide.

DISASTROUS EXPEDITIONS

It takes guts to set off into the unknown and explore the wilderness. Today's explorers may have radio backup and support, but in the old days it was man against nature, one to one. Often it was nature that won.

THE ORDEAL

In 1860, the explorers Robert O'Hara Burke and William John Wills left Melbourne, Australia, to cross the parched heartlands of the country by camel. They almost succeeded, but the return journey was disastrous. There were deaths, arguments and missed meetings and a lack of supplies meant they had to eat camel, snakes and seeds that made them ill. Both explorers died, Burke under this tree, and only one team member returned to tell the story.

AN AWFUL PLACE...

In 1910–1912, Robert Falcon Scott led a British expedition to the South Pole. The explorers were brave, but it all went horribly wrong. Their motor sledges were useless and the ponies had to be shot. A Norwegian team, led by Roald Amundsen, reached the Pole just before them. "Great God! This is an awful place," wrote Scott in his diary. On the return journey, the weather worsened and they ran short of food and fuel. One man died after cracking his head. Another caught frostbite. Not one of them made it back to base.

NO SURVIVORS

In 1845, a British naval expedition set out for the Canadian Arctic, looking for new shipping routes. The expedition was led by Sir John Franklin, but he and all his crew disappeared. It seems the ships became locked in the ice. The explorers made island camps for the winter, but many of the sailors became sick from pneumonia and died. Today, modern icebreakers like this one keep the shipping lanes open.

WATCH OUT!

In 1848, a few surviving crew members from Sir John Franklin's expedition made a bid to escape overland. They starved and even resorted to cannibalism in a vain bid to stay alive.

MYTHOLOGICAL MONSTERS

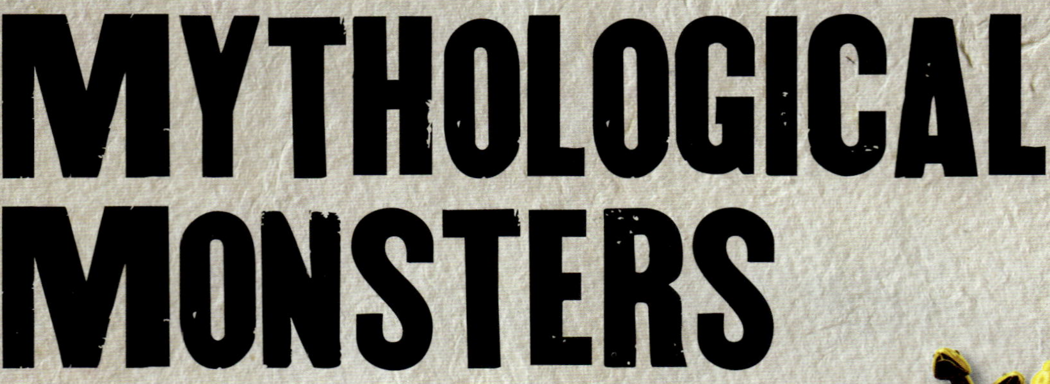

The myths of ancient Greece and Rome are the stuff of nightmares. They tell of terrifying monsters and vengeful gods.

THREE HEADS

Beware the jaws of Cerberus, the hound of hell who guarded the gates of the Underworld, home to the dead. With his three heads, he could see the past, present and future. Cerberus snarled, slavered and slobbered and had a taste for living flesh. He only allowed in the souls of the dead, and made sure that none of these ever left.

DON'T LOOK NOW!

Medusa was a monster, a Gorgon with a writhing tangle of hissing snakes in place of hair. Anyone who looked into her eyes was turned to stone. She was beheaded by the hero Perseus, who then used her head as a weapon.

AMAZING!

DODGY DNA

Cerberus's mother was Echidna, who was half snake and half woman. His father was Typhon, a terrifying giant who breathed fire.

DID YOU KNOW?

HORRID HARPIES

The Harpies were winged creatures, sometimes shown as terrible hags with wings and talons. They snatched food, spread filth and caused famine.

THE MINOTAUR

On the island of Crete there was a maze called the Labyrinth. Trapped at its heart was a bellowing, raging monster, half man and half bull, called the Minotaur. Every seven years this beast ate seven youths and seven maidens, specially sent from Athens. It was slain by a hero named Theseus.

DID YOU KNOW?

SIREN SONGS

The Sirens were water nymphs. Passing sailors who heard their sweet song became drowsy and dreamy and were unaware that they were being lured to a terrible death.

MAN-EATER

The cyclopes were gruesome, one-eyed giants armed with clubs. The most famous was Polyphemus, who captured the Greek hero Odysseus and his friends and trapped them in his cave. Odysseus attacked and blinded the giant, plunging a burning stake into his one eye.

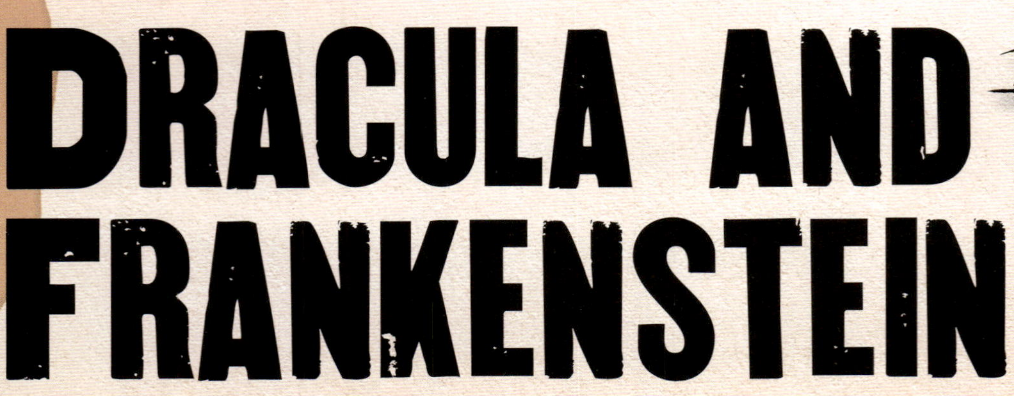

DRACULA AND FRANKENSTEIN

Vampires and crazed monsters are the subject of many folk tales, superstitions and legends and have fuelled the imagination of writers and film makers.

BLOODSUCKERS

A belief in vampires was common in the 1700s and 1800s, especially in regions of southeastern Europe, such as Transylvania, in Romania. Country folk claimed that vampires really existed and that these 'undead' sucked the blood from animals and humans with their fangs. Anyone bitten by a vampire would become one themselves.

FRANKENSTEIN'S MONSTER

Frankenstein was one of the first-ever science fiction novels. Written in 1817 by English author Mary Shelley, it tells the story of a student, Victor Frankenstein, who creates a living being from bits of corpses and brings it to life. The creature is treated very unkindly by humans and seeks furious revenge on its maker. Recreated in countless theatre, film and television adaptations, this story has been giving people the shivers ever since.

GOTHIC HORROR

In many modern film and television tales of vampires, we see a coffin lid creak open deep in a burial vault in some ruined castle. Out of it steps a pale figure in a billowing black cloak. This person sets out into the night with a deadly mission, to fasten their teeth into the throat of an innocent victim, until bloated with blood. Such tales are mostly based on the gothic novel *Dracula*, written by the Irish novelist, Bram Stoker, in 1897.

COOL FACT!

KEEP OFF!

It was believed that the only things that would keep vampires at bay were garlands of garlic or Christian crucifixes, and the only way to kill a vampire? A stake driven through the heart while the vampire slept.

FIT FOR VAMPIRES

The name Dracula was taken from the Draculesti, the princes of Wallachia, Romania, in the 1400s. One of them, Vlad III, impaled thousands of his enemies on wooden stakes. Bran Castle, situated on the border between Transylvania and Wallachia, is one of several castles claiming links with the Dracula story.

ZOMBIES AND WEREWOLVES

Creatures of the night, rotting corpses brought back to life, bloodthirsty shape-shifters... The worst fears of our ancestors are kept alive in modern horror movies.

WEREWOLVES

Fear of werewolves dates back to Greek and Roman times and was common in Europe during the Middle Ages. A werewolf was a person who could turn him or herself into a huge wolf and then turn back into their human form. As a wolf, the creature was said to hunt children, raid graveyards and behave in a terrifying and destructive manner.

GHASTLY GHOULS

The word 'ghoul' comes from the Arabic for 'seizer' or 'demon'. Originally, ghouls were believed to be evil spirits that lurked in the desert. They could take on the shape of hyenas, seizing and attacking travellers and then crunching up their bodies and bones. Sometimes they would take on the shape of the person they had just eaten.

ZOMBIES

Followers of the West African religion known as vodun or voodoo believe that sorcerers can bring dead people back to life and keep them under their control. Meet the undead, or 'zombies'. Such beliefs passed from Africa to the Caribbean, especially to Haiti. The Haitian lord of death is known as Baron Samedi. Only his magic can stop dead bodies being turned into zombies. Mass zombie horror has become a feature of many modern movies and cults.

SPIRITS OF EVIL

In the days when people believed in witches, they also believed in 'familiar spirits'. These were agents of the Devil, who helped the witches do evil. They might take the form of demons, toads, crows, hares or black cats.

Haiti's lord of death, Baron Samedi, is often shown as a scary skeleton wearing a top hat.

DID YOU KNOW?

HOWLING AT THE MOON

In many modern werewolf tales, when the werewolf turns into their wolf form, they can be heard howling eerily at the full moon. Real wolves are often more active on bright, clear nights, which is probably where the idea of howling at the moon came from. In modern tales and horror films, a werewolf can only be killed with a silver bullet.

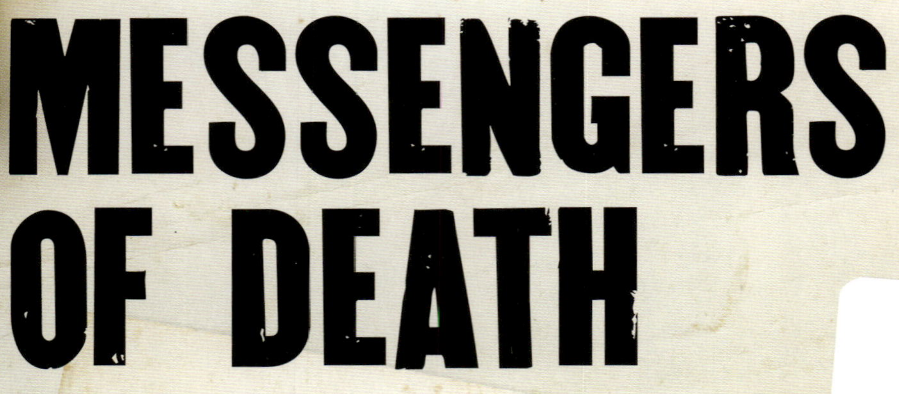

MESSENGERS OF DEATH

Sometimes people believe they have been warned, by a spirit or messenger of death, that they will soon die. It's enough to make your blood run cold!

If you see your double (in German, your *Doppelgänger*) walking towards you, watch out! Some say this is an omen of your own death.

WAIL OF THE BANSHEE

A banshee is a female spirit of the Celtic lands, who signals the approach of death with an unearthly wail that rises and falls in the night. Sometimes she may be seen washing bloodstained clothes. The banshee is regarded as one of the fairy folk, but may also be linked to ancient beliefs in the Morrigan, an Irish goddess who flies over warriors slaughtered in battle, in the form of a crow.

DID YOU KNOW?

YAMA

In the Hindu religion, Yama is the much-feared god of death. Nobody can stop him coming, or change the timing of his visit. His two dogs, each with four eyes and wide nostrils, guard the road to his abode.

HOUNDS OF HELL

Imagine a ghostly dog with a hairy black coat and burning red eyes, prowling through the night and howling, before vanishing into the shadows. According to the folklore of many lands, just a glimpse of this hell-hound can be a warning of death to come.

AMAZING!

DANCE OF DEATH

In the Middle Ages, many pictures show Death leading his victims away from the living world in a 'dance of death'. Nobody can escape his bony grasp, young or old, rich or poor.

THE GRIM REAPER

From the 15th century onward, the figure of Death was shown as a skeleton wrapped in a black, hooded robe. Often his face could not be seen. He carried a scythe, to show that his job was to cut the ties between a person's soul and their body. Sometimes he was also shown carrying an hourglass, to show that a person's time on Earth had run out.

INDEX

INDEX

PICTURE CREDITS

tr = top right; br = bottom right; tl = top left; bl = bottom left; tc = top centre; bc = bottom centre; lc = left centre rc = right centre; c = centre; main = main image

p11, tr, Operation Deep Scope 2005 Expedition: NOAA Office of Ocean Exploration; p12, tr. Acatenazzi; p16, tr. unknown; p17, bl. Franz Eugen Köhler; p18, cr. Ingemar Johansson; p18, cr. Peter Woodard, p23; main. Foter.com / CC BY-SA; p24, cr. Ryane Snow; p41, tl. Hadal; p42, bl. artist unknown; p43, bl. Anagoria; p66, cr. Summum; p50, bl. Roman Klementschitz; p68, main. Pattymooney; p72, bl. Willem Swanenburgh, cr. Wikipedia, Kim Traynor; p79, br. C.G. Newhall; p86/87, Ben-Zin; p81, lc. Chagai. tl. Wikipedia, Suizaperuana; p84, bl. Peterdownunder

Thinkstock

p6, br; p6/7, main; p7, br; p90, tr; p33, tl; p93, tc.

All other images courtesy of Shutterstock

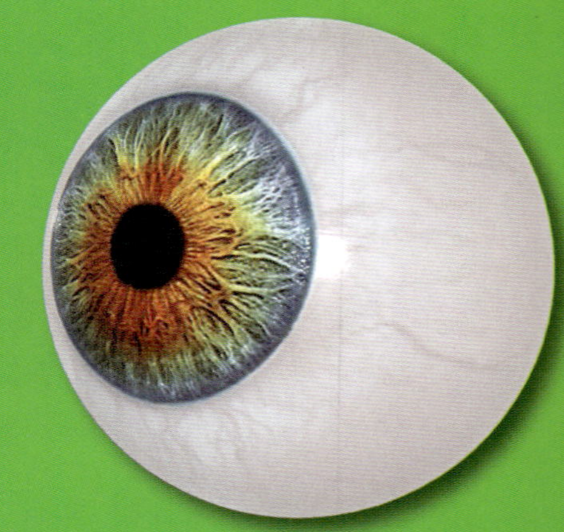

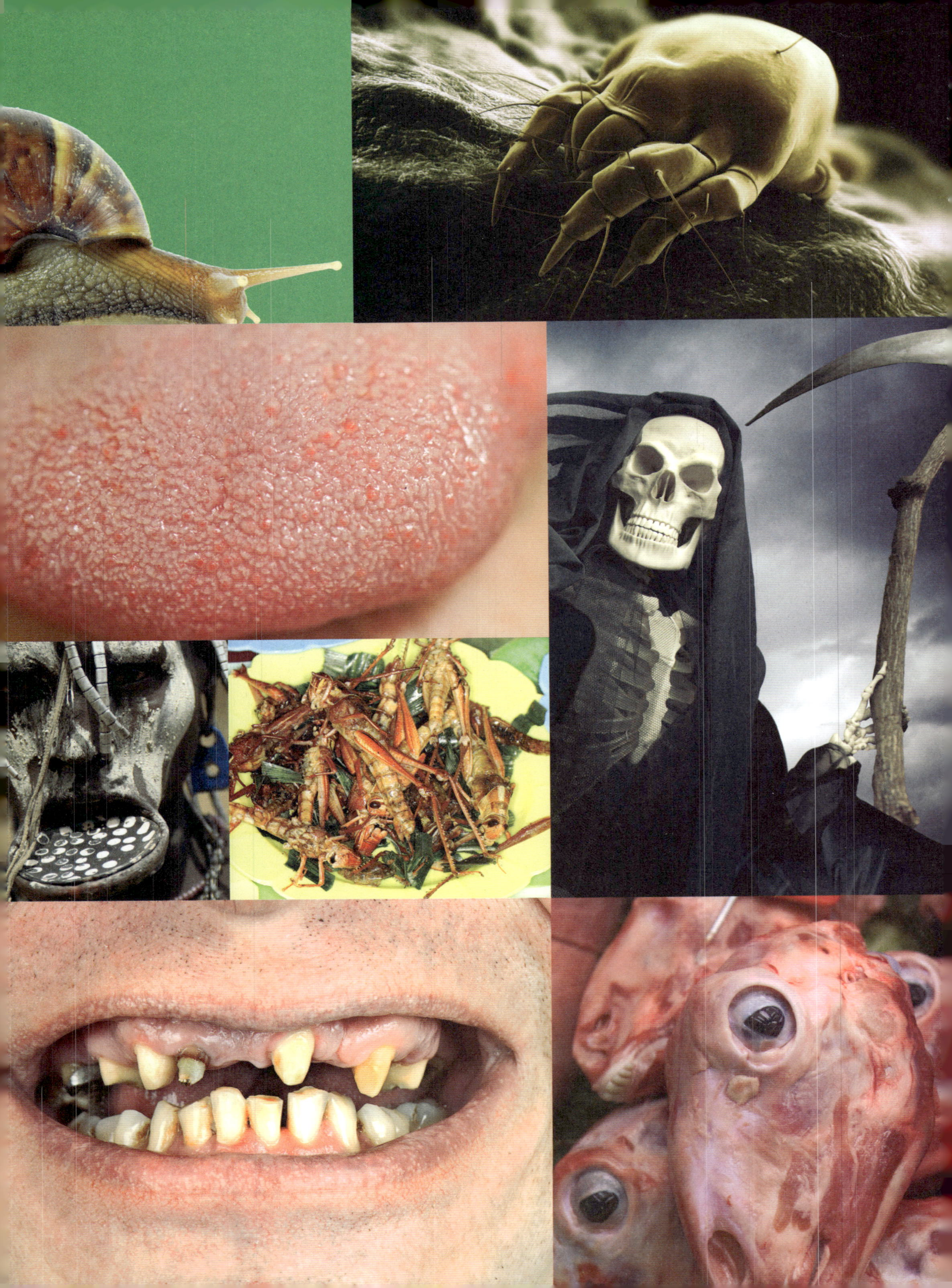